Everyman's Poetry

*Everyman, I will go with thee,
and be thy guide*

Alexander Pushkin

Selected and edited by A. D. P. BRIGGS

University of Birmingham

D1444414

EVERYMAN

J. M. Dent · London

This edition first published by Everyman Paperbacks in 1997
Introduction and other critical apparatus © J. M. Dent 1997

All rights reserved

J. M. Dent
Orion Publishing Group
Orion House
5 Upper St Martin's Lane
London WC2H 9EA

Typeset by Deltatype Ltd, Birkenhead, Merseyside
Printed in Great Britain by
The Guernsey Press Co. Ltd, Guernsey, C. I.

British Library Cataloguing-in-Publication Data
is available upon request.

ISBN 0 460 87862 X

Contents

Note on the Author and Editor

ALEXANDER SERGEYEVICH PUSHKIN, born in Moscow on 26 May 1799, came to prominence in 1820 with his first long poem, *Ruslan and Lyudmila*. Exiled to the south of Russia, he wrote *The Captive in the Caucasus* and began *Yevgeny Onegin*, a novel in verse. Allowed to return north, he remained in exile at Mikhaylovskoye during 1824–5, the period of *The Gypsies, Count Nulin* and the Shakespearean play, *Boris Godunov*. After 1825 he lived in Moscow, paying an extended visit to Transcaucasia in 1829, where he saw military action against the Turks. He married Natalya Goncharova in 1831, the year in which he also completed *Yevgeny Onegin*. A long journey to the Urals in 1833 provided materials for his historical tale, *The Captain's Daughter* (1833–5). His finest narrative poem, *The Bronze Horseman*, was written in 1833, along with his best-known prose tale, *The Queen of Spades*. Two unhappy years in St Petersburg (1834–6), involving humiliation in court circles, mounting debts and little creative work, culminated in scandalous rumours concerning his wife, which could be resolved only by a duel, in which he was mortally wounded on 27 January 1837.

Universally acknowledged as Russia's greatest poet, Pushkin set the standards and provided models which have formed and directed the national literature ever since. The Russian language itself was reformed by his innovatory use of it. His eight hundred lyrics, numerous narrative poems, tales in verse and prose, historical and critical articles, along with his collected letters, comprise the richest single treasure-house in Russian culture. His works have inspired thousands of musical versions, including several famous operas.

A. D. P. BRIGGS, Professor of Russian Language and Literature at the University of Birmingham, is a specialist in modern Russian literature, mainly of the nineteenth century. Among his many publications are six books, three of them devoted to Alexander Pushkin. His current work is on Pushkin and music.

Chronology of Pushkin's Life

Year	Age	Life
1799		26 May: Born in Moscow
1800–11	1–11	Grows up without parental affection, entrusted to nursemaids, French tutors and governesses. Lazy, but an avid, precocious reader. Learns Russian from household serfs and especially his nanny, Arina Rodionovna

Chronology of his Times

Year	Artistic Context	Historical Events
1798		Napoleon captures Malta and invades Egypt
		French fleet defeated by Nelson at Battle of the Nile
1799	Birth of Balzac	French occupy Naples and Zurich
		Napoleon defeats Turks; made First Consul
		Death of George Washington
1800		Austrians defeated by Napoleon at Marengo
1801	Chateaubriand, *Atala*	Murder of Tsar Paul; accession of Alexander I
1802	Death of Radishchev, author of *A Journey from St Petersburg to Moscow*	Napoleon made First Consul for life
	Birth of Hugo	France annexes Piedmont
	Mme de Staël, *Delphine*	
	Chateaubriand, *René*	
1803	Death of Bogdanovich, poet, author of *Dushen'ka*	Great Britain declares war against France
1804	Birth of George Sand	Napoleon becomes Emperor
	Death of Kant	
1805	Death of Schiller	Battles of Trafalgar and Austerlitz
1806		Battle of Jena; Napoleon occupies Berlin
1807	Mme de Staël, *Corinne*	Battle of Friedland; Russians defeated by Napoleon
1808	Scott, *Marmion*	Napoleon enters Rome
	Goethe, *Faust*, Part One	Wellington enters Spain
		Siege of Saragossa

Year	Age	Life
1811–17	11–17	Studies at the new lycée of Tsarskoye Selo, near St Petersburg

Year	Artistic Context	Historical Events
1809	Birth of Gogol. Krylov first book of fables	Battle of Corunna; death of Sir John Moore
1810	Birth of Musset Mme de Staël, *De l'Allemagne*	France annexes Holland
1811	Zhukovsky, *Svetlana* Austen, *Sense and Sensibility* Byron, *Childe Harold's Pilgrimage*, Cantos One and Two Birth of Belinsky, radical literary critic	
1812		Napoleon declares war on Russia; battle of Borodino French defeat Russians; burning of Moscow, followed by Napoleon's retreat
1813	Austen, *Pride and Prejudice* Byron, *The Giaour*	Wellington invades France
1814	Birth of Lermontov Scott, *Waverley*	Allied sovereigns enter Paris Napoleon deposed, banished to Elba
1815		British defeated at Battle of New Orleans Napoleon returns to Paris Defeat of Napoleon at Battle of Waterloo Allies enter Paris Napoleon sent to St Helena
1816	Deaths of the poet Derzhavin and dramatist Ozerov Byron, *The Prisoner of Chillon* Coleridge, *Christabel* Constant, *Adolphe* Goethe, *Italienische Reise*	

Year	Age	Life
1817–20	17–20	Undemanding government post in St Petersburg. Dissipated life style; some links with revolutionary young people. Some unpublishable liberal poems circulate in manuscript
1820	20	*Ruslan and Lyudmila*. Exiled to Yekaterinoslav; transferred to Kishinev
1821	21	*The Captive in the Caucasus, The Robber Brothers*
1822	22	*The Fountain of Bakhchisaray*
1823	23	Begins *Yevgeny Onegin*. Transferred to Odessa
1824	24	Returns north to internal exile at Mikhaylovskoye. *The Gypsies*
1825	25	*Count Nulin, Boris Godunov*. Freed from exile, but with Nicholas I as personal censor in Moscow
1828	28	*Poltava*
1829	29	Visits Transcaucasia; action against the Turks
1830	30	Stranded at Boldino by cholera outbreak. *The Little House in Kolomna, Little Tragedies, Tales of Belkin*

Year	Artistic Context	Historical Events
1817	Byron, *Manfred* and remainder of *Childe Harold's Pilgrimage*	
1818	Birth of Turgenev Death of satirical journalist, Novikov Byron, *Beppo*	
1819	Byron, *Don Juan*, Cantos One and Two Stendhal, *De l'Amour*	Florida ceded to USA by Spain Birth of future Queen Victoria
1820	Lamartine, *Premières Méditations* Shelley, *Prometheus Unbound*	Naples; Carbonari revolt
1821	Births of Dostoyevsky, Baudelaire and Flaubert Death of Keats	Austrians occupy Naples Death of Napoleon
1822	Death of Shelley	Greek Declaration of Independence
1823	Lamartine, *Nouvelles Méditations*	French invade Spain
1824	Byron, remainder of *Don Juan* Death of Byron Griboyedov, *Woe from Wit*	
1825	Death of poet and revolutionary Ryleyev (executed) Death of Karamzin	Death of Alexander I; accession of Nicholas I Ruthless suppression of Decembrist uprising
1827	Death of Blake Manzoni, *I Promessi Sposi*	Kingdom of Greece founded
1828	Birth of Leo Tolstoy	Russia declares war against Turkey
1829	Death of Griboyedov Balzac, *Les Chouans*	Andrew Jackson US President
1830	Battle of *Hernani*	Death of George IV; accession of William IV Louis Philippe proclaimed King of France

Year	Age	Life
1831	31	18 February: marries Natalya Goncharova. 5 October: completes *Yevgeny Onegin*
1833	33	Travels east to the Urals, engaged in historical research. Second 'Boldino Autumn'. *Andzhelo, The Bronze Horseman, The Queen of Spades*
1833–5	33–5	*The Captain's Daughter*
1833–6	33–6	Unhappy period in St Petersburg. Humiliation in court circles, mounting debts, jealousy of wife's admirers. Little creative work done
1837	37	Goaded by scandalous rumours into a duel with Georges D'Anthès, adopted son of Dutch ambassador. 27 January: Pushkin wounded in the stomach in duel with D'Anthès; dies two days later

Year	Artistic Context	Historical Events
1831	Death of Hegel Stendhal, *Le Rouge et le Noir*	Poles defeat Russians at Grochow
1832	Goethe, *Faust*, Part Two Deaths of Goethe and Scott	Poland annexed by Russia
1833	Heine, *Die romantische Schule*	Slavery abolished in British colonies
1834	Death of Coleridge	
1837		Death of William IV; accession of Queen Victoria

Introduction

The time-honoured way of getting to know a poet's work is simply to browse among his pages. This approach will suit Alexander Pushkin; reading a dozen of his poems at random will deliver a good general impression of his work. But anyone who wishes to take matters further may benefit from a more systematic approach, designed to cover in some detail most aspects of Pushkin's versatile writing. This selection has been arranged for such a person, who would do well to read closely one or two of Pushkin's poems presenting more than a single theme and then to follow up their ideas in other works. Even in translation it will be interesting to keep an eye also on poetic form, over which he exercises unusually skilful control.

'Winter. What shall we do out in the country . . . ?' is particularly useful in this respect, and consequently it appears first. Such priority is well-deserved; few poems exemplify Pushkin's manner and ideas more comprehensively. All the events and preoccupations described in it occurred in real life – a useful reminder that many of Pushkin's poems are of biographical interest. 'Winter . . .' addresses three themes in some detail. First, winter in the Russian backwoods, with its brief excitements followed by boredom and petty distractions. (Comparison may be made with Pope's *Epistle to Miss Blount*, who has to 'count the slow clock and dine exact at noon'). Second, literature; reading and writing (especially poetry) were Pushkin's life-blood, though in the middle of this poem much is to be learned from his description of what it feels like *not* to be inspired. Third, a love affair, all the way from light flirtation to sensuous physical contact; the poem breaks off deliciously in mid-couplet (an almost unnoticeable literary joke) inviting you to imagine your own culmination . . . We know what happened in real life since the poet later describes waking up next day with the same girl to a beautiful dawn (see *Winter Morning*). All in all, this is a good start to Pushkin: his own life, Russia, nature, poetry, love and sex – most of his work comes under one or other of these headings.

'Winter . . .' also indulges in some clever stylistic tricks, a number of which easily survive translation. The poet uses a long, formal line (the hexameter), noble and heroic, but everything that he does with it is deliberately wrong. He fails to observe the statutory pauses in mid-line and at line-ends. The poem begins with two strong examples of enjambement, the like of which brought the house down in Paris at Hugo's drama the 'Battle of *Hernani*' in 1830, though Pushkin's poem is earlier. And what about the subject matter? Servants, cups of tea, the weather – these low-born newcomers to Russian poetry arrive in such a stately vehicle (seated on top of a poem in classical hexameters – Alexandrines to the French) that they enjoy the cheeky jauntiness of ragamuffins leading the Lord Mayor's Parade. Several important points arise here: the ordinariness of much of Pushkin's subject-matter, his astute mastery of technique and, conversely, a casual attitude to his trade, good-humoured and balancing on the brink of parody.

In the next poem, *Autumn* – another masterpiece on more than one theme – a dozen *ottava rima* stanzas tell us amusingly of Pushkin's attitude to the various seasons and why he was particularly inspired by autumn. Towards the end it emerges that this latter point is the purpose of the poem, which is about poetic inspiration, now at its most positive and powerful. (Again this is real life; Pushkin spent two amazingly productive autumns at his Boldino estate in 1830 and 1833, when this poem was completed.) Pushkin is usually wary of metaphor, preferring straightforward description, well-supported by magically appropriate language. But, like a true master of his craft, he can turn on spectacular effects when they are needed. *Autumn* contains a couple of his most striking extended similes: the season is like a beautiful but moribund consumptive girl (stanza 6); poetry is like a sleeping galleon ready to put on sail when inspiration blows up (stanza 11). (Through its visual imagery the concluding stanza recalls Wordsworth's sonnet, 'With ships the sea was sprinkled far and nigh . . .'.) In Pushkin's poem, the poignancy of the former image is sharpened by prosaic language and multiple enjambement. The entire stanza, even with its triple rhymes, reads like ordinary speech, and any translation should attempt to convey that quality of ordinariness. Many of the poems in this volume, including *Autumn*, have been retranslated, partly to ensure that interesting formal properties like these are not lost.

After reading 'Winter . . .' and *Autumn* the reader knows a good deal about Pushkin and, like the galleon, can sail off anywhere. The poems which follow are grouped roughly thematically, rather than chronologically, in the order already encountered in 'Winter . . .'. Following a number of personal poems, autobiographical but enjoyable without a detailed knowledge of Pushkin's life-story (pp. 7–14), are the three groups introduced by 'Winter . . .': poems about the natural world (pp. 14–22), poetry (pp. 22–5) and love (pp. 26–37). These are succeeded by some poems of ideas, from the lightly philosophical to the overtly political (pp. 38–47). The groupings are not intended to be rigidly schematic – there are many poems covering more than one subject which cannot easily be categorised – but they should help to illustrate what Pushkin had to say, and how his ideas developed, in several areas of interest. Within the groupings, poems do appear for the most part in chronological order.

A few poems are particular favourites of the Russians, and thus not to be missed. Among the personal poems *Remembrance* and *Elegy* stand out for two reasons. In Russian they are full of the most delicate and impressive sound patterns, and they both express a philosophy of life which is truly Pushkinian. In each poem the writer surveys his past life, loathing what he recalls, but remains determined to carry on the struggle of human existence. By a small margin the positive outweighs the negative; the fundamental goodness of being cannot be controverted. In a late (undated) poem, 'The time has come, dear friend. My heart now longs for peace', Pushkin captures an escapist mood which probably everyone will recognise. Nature is best represented in Pushkin's longer works, especially his novel in verse *Yevgeny Onegin*, but many of his lyrics touch on the subject. *Winter Morning* is recommended in its own right and as a follow-up to 'Winter . . .'. In *The Caucasus* Pushkin gives an expressive account of the beauty of that region. In *Demons* he depicts the frightful peril of the Russian winter, using motifs from Russian folklore; the original is characterised by sounds so weird and ominous that their uncanny music matters more than the words. Of the poems on poetry both *The Prophet* and *Exegi Monumentum* convey Pushkin's view of the importance and magnificence of the poet's function. The former (an adaptation of passages from *Isaiah*) deals ostensibly with the conversion of an ordinary man into an Old Testament prophet, but this is generally taken as a metaphor for poetic inspiration. Pushkin wrote dozens of excellent love poems; among the finest are 'Oh, I have loved you . . .', *To Anna Kern*, 'Towards the shores of your far homeland' and 'No, not for me the stormiest pleasures of the senses', which was so openly personal and sexual that it was not published during the poet's lifetime.

Two small poems in this group will be of interest to music-lovers. *The Singer* (written when Pushkin was 17) provides the words for the lovely opening duet between the two sisters in Tchaikovsky's *Yevgeny Onegin*; *Gypsy Girl's Song* is an extract from Pushkin's narrative poem *The Gypsies*, one which shows that the librettists of Bizet's *Carmen* used that poem as part of the basis for the opera, since some of its key words ('Coupe-moi, brûle-moi') are sung by the heroine. Among the remaining lyrics *The Upas Tree* stands out for its remarkable depiction of the human propensity for violence (and is curiously similar to Blake's *Poison Tree*); *The Waggon of Life* for its jocular view of our brief life-span expressed in *risqué* language unusable until recent times in both Russia and England; and 'Gift of life so useless, why . . .' as a pessimistic (Lermontov-like) attitude to the gift of existence. *Verses composed during a sleepless night*, beautiful in itself, will be recognised by many who have been enchanted by its setting for soprano by Benjamin Britten (1965). Pushkin's commitment to the liberal cause in his country is seen in two political poems, both addressed to members of the ill-fated Decembrist revolutionaries of 1825: 'Deep down in your Siberian mine . . .' and *Arion*. A few lines of blank verse from his play *Boris Godunov*, better known in Mussorgsky's operatic version, are also included; Pimen's monologue is known by all Russians.

Pushkin's finest single achievement is *Yevgeny Onegin*. Written in 366 sonnet-like stanzas, this famous story describes the ill-matched and ill-starred Yevgeny and Tatyana, the death in a duel by Onegin's hand of Vladimir Lensky, and a huge slice of Russian rural and urban life. It is also something of a guide to world literature, with its multiple references, serious and jocular, direct and oblique, to dozens of writers from many countries. A few stanzas from the end of the novel are included here in order to give a general impression of how the novel works.

Three narrative poems complete the volume. *The Captive in the Caucasus* was Pushkin's first real narrative poem, written in 1820–21 under the influence of Byron. It has its weaknesses – some vagueness in characterisation and lack of incident – but it also contains vivid descriptions of the same bellicose Caucasian mountain-folk who are still at the centre of conflict today in Chechnya, and also of the impressive natural scenery. *The Godyssey, or The Deviliad* (known in Russian as *Gavriiliada* after the Angel Gabriel) is an overtly sacrilegious re-enactment of several Bible stories (Adam and Eve, Joseph and Mary, the Annunciation, etc.) run together into an extended sexual romp. In its day Pushkin could not acknowledge authorship; neither could Russian criticism until recently. *The Godyssey* is presented now as a demonstration of Pushkin's humour and the delight which he took in matters sexual; in this preoccupation he stands alongside writers such as Chaucer and his much-admired Shakespeare. *The Bronze Horseman* is acknowledged as a true Russian masterpiece, Pushkin's finest work apart from *Yevgeny Onegin*. Although the sound effects of this poem – its most formidable quality in the original – are difficult to convey in translation, the story, characters and ideas survive that process rather better. The issues at stake in this poem are large ones, concerning Russian politics and history, human destiny and our smallness, insignificance and vulnerability *vis-à-vis* the mighty power of the universe and the elements. At a lower level of significance, the tale itself is full of human interest and endearing detail; the poet has come a long way from the less consequential open stretches of *The Captive in the Caucasus.*

Although the Russian and English languages have much in common (especially an impressive energy based on strong word stress which is lacking in, for instance, French), they also differ a good deal. English likes snappy monosyllables and not too many consonants in close proximity; Russian loves to stretch itself out in luxurious polysyllabic phrases with much clustering of consonants. With its thirty-letter alphabet, including ten vowels and a group of exuberant Slavonic consonants, Russian may fairly lay claim to be Europe's most expressive tongue. The musical potential of these generous resources makes the task of learning this language worthwhile in itself. Poetry-lovers should consider undertaking it, using Pushkin's poetry (and prose) to assist them. These points were well-made by Anthony Burgess, who went so far as to recommend that everyone should learn 'Oh, I have loved you . . .' in Russian ('Ya vas lyubil . . .') phonetically, bit by bit, in order to appreciate sound values, poetry and the Russian language.

Alexander Pushkin virtually created this language in its modern form, bringing together for the first time the scattered linguistic potential bequeathed by his predecessors. He showed how it was possible for grand and sonorous Old Slavonic to blend with rough vernacular Russian and for both of them to be modernised and civilised by graceful Gallic sensibility. The secret, for him, was easy; all he had to do was to keep things simple and use the right word in the right place. Archaisms appear in *The Prophet*; everyday colloquialisms in 'Winter. What shall we do . . . ?'; folkloric language in *Demons*; swearwords in *The Waggon of Life*; semi-scientific expressions help with geography and ethnic tradition in *The Captive in the Caucasus*; a spirit of neutral modern prose seems to convert itself naturally into verses when that is all that is needed – as in *Autumn* and 'Oh, I have loved you . . .'. In Pushkin's greatest works, particularly *The Bronze Horseman* and *Yevgeny Onegin*, most of these registers come together in what would appear as a dazzling display of linguistic virtuosity if it were not so well-modulated by an easy instinct for choosing words appropriately. It is for these qualities that Pushkin is hailed as the father of the modern Russian language and literature. Not all of them are lost in translation.

A. D. P. BRIGGS

Note on the Translations and Translators

The first translations of Pushkin's works into English began to appear while he was still alive and continued to be published in various journals throughout the nineteenth century. There are now hundreds of translations to choose from and their production continues today at an encouraging rate. Styles of translation vary considerably, from the rigidly accurate (sometimes resulting in unpoetic or archaic versions) to the free-flowing and imaginative (which can risk failure to give a clear impression of how Pushkin sounds in the original). In selecting for this edition an attempt has been made to include poems which read like poetry and also like Pushkin.

The form of the original has been closely followed. Metres and rhyme schemes are considered important and have generally been preserved. The ordering of rhymes often contains something of interest or significance. For instance, the irregularity of the rhyme scheme in *Verses composed during a sleepless night* reflects the poet's restlessness at that time and should on no account be smoothed into neat stanzas. (There are fifteen lines in this poem, but translators have often shortened it to a more usual fourteen.) Similarly, some sections of *The Bronze Horseman* depend for their full effect on strict regularity (the opening ten lines, rhyming aabab twice) or the very opposite, as at the onset of the hero's madness, when a run of nineteen lines built on only seven rhymes refuses to settle into anything like good order. Hidden subtleties like these – and there are many of them – ought not to be sacrificed.

Faithfulness to the original has been disregarded in one important area, also concerned with rhyme. Pushkin's verse almost invariably alternates single-syllable rhymes with two-syllable ones (masculine with feminine). The latter are not easy to find in English without recourse to participles (singing/bringing) or hackneyed formulas (ocean/motion). They have therefore been dispensed with on a regular basis in the three narrative poems included in this edition and also longer poems like 'Winter. What shall we do . . . ?' and *Autumn*. In this respect the shorter lyrics vary. Sometimes the alternation of masculine and feminine rhymes has emerged naturally, thus preserving the exact rhythm of the original; on other occasions strenuous efforts to ensure this alternation (which is rare in English poetry) have not seemed necessary. Since even a good translation can be reduced to banality through the use of rhymes which are too easy and familiar, a measure of approximate rhyming has been allowed. This slight anachronism permits a greater possibility of recapturing the freshness of Pushkin's own poetry through versions which are accurate without being commonplace or tedious.

Five translators provide the bulk of this volume, with five other sources making smaller contributions. They are as follows:

anon   24
Hon. M. Baring   51, 52
A. D. P. Briggs   1, 2, 3, 4, 5, 6, 8, 9, 11, 14, 20, 23, 28, 30, 32, 33, 35, 38, 39, 40, 42, 43, 44, 46, 47, 48, 50, 54, 55, 56, 58, 59, 60
C. M. Bowra   7, 10, 15, 18, 19, 21, 26, 29
F. Cornford   16
B. Deutsch   12, 34, 41, 49, 53
O. Elton   57 (revised by A. D. P. Briggs)
W. Morrison   17, 22, 25, 31, 37
P. Selver   13
I. Zheleznova   27, 36, 45

All translations are accredited within the text. Where no translator is given, the translation is the work of A. D. P. Briggs.

Alexander Pushkin

1 'Winter. What shall we do out in the country?'

Winter. What shall we do out in the country? I greet
My servant as he brings my morning cup of tea
With questions. Is it cold outside? Has it stopped snowing?
Is there a covering? Should I perhaps get going,
Go for a ride – or stay in bed all day and labour
Through these old magazines passed on by a kind neighbour?
There is fresh snow, so up we get, and we're away –
A muffled clip-clop trot; the light of early day.
Wielding our riding-crops, off with the dogs we fly
To search the pale snow with a scrutinising eye. 10
We wheel across the countryside, till late we roam,
Then – two missed hares behind us – suddenly we're home.
This is the life! As night falls, to the blizzard's howl,
The candle gutters, and my heart shrinks. All is foul.
I drink the boredom down, slow poison, drop by drop.
Let me try reading. No, the letters blur – I stop.
My thoughts have wandered miles away. The book snaps
　　shut.
I sit down, seize the pen, cajoling my muse, but
She is too sleepy, all her words have lost their hold.
The sounds won't come together. I have no control 20
Over my handmaid, Rhyme, strange girl. My words go wrong.
My cold and misty lines drag their slow length along.
I weary of my lyre, with both of us so fractious.
Out in the drawing-room, what topics now distract us?
The sugar-works and the municipal election . . .
My hostess apes the weather in sourness of complexion.
Her speedy, steely needles clack, and then she starts
A little fortune-telling with the King of Hearts.
Oh aching boredom! How the days drag, far from town!
But, if, in this sad hamlet, as the night comes down, 30
When I sit playing draughts tucked quietly away,
Perhaps there should arrive a carriage, or a sleigh,
Bringing chance visitors thrown suddenly amidst us,

A mother and her girls (two blonde and shapely sisters!),
Then how the backwoods stir – what life this visit brings!
The world, because of it, brims over with good things!
The eyes meet first in angled-lingering observation
And then a word or two leads on to conversation,
Warm laughter and an evening singing with the sisters,
With whirling waltzes, secret dinner-table whispers,   40
Long, languid glances mixed with bantering repartee,
Protracted meetings on the close stairs, she with me . . .
On to the twilit balcony at last she sneaks,
Her neck, her bosom bared, the snowstorm at her cheeks.
But northern storms can never harm a Russian rose!
Her warm kiss sears the frosty night, her ardour glows.
O lovely Russian girl, snow-silvered and so cool! . . .

                                                (1829)

2   Autumn

(A Fragment)

'What does not at this time enter my drowsing mind?' – *Derzhavin*

1

October's here again. The trees will soon have tossed
The last leaves down from their bare branches. Now the chill
Of Autumn breathes on us. The road is hard with frost.
Although the stream still courses, babbling past the mill,
The pond is frozen over. Galloping across
The open fields, my neighbour tastes again the thrill
Of chasing; fine the sport, and bruised the winter wheat.
His baying hounds arouse the woodlands from their sleep.

2

This is the time for me! Springtime I can't abide,
With all that smelly thawing slush. My spirits yearn,   10
My blood seethes, my heart aches and I feel ill inside.
I'm altogether happier with Winter stern.

I love the snowy waste, the sleigh, the moonlit ride
So fast and free, when you sit cuddling your girl.
Her face is warm and fresh, her sable glistens black.
You squeeze her hand, she squeezes passionately back.

3

Oh for the bladed boots! How good to pull them on,
Down by the solid river, and skate upon the glass!
And what about the games, that special winter fun? . . .
Yes, but . . . Snow follows snow till half a year has passed.   20
And, long before that, even Bruin, the shaggy one,
Grows weary in his lair. You get fed up at last
Of sleighing with the sirens ever and again
Or moping by the stove and at the window-pane.

4

Summer! I might have loved you like a precious jewel,
But for the stifling heat, the dust, the gnats, the flies.
You desiccate the mind, your days are long and cruel.
We suffer with the arid landscape as it dies,
We are obsessed with drinking, finding something cool,
And soon we think of Mistress Winter's sad demise.   30
We packed her off with wine and pancakes. Very nice,
But now we call her back with ice-cream treats and ice.

5

The closing days of Autumn are often not held dear,
But this is just the time by which I am beguiled.
It glows with modesty; its beauty is austere.
In nature's family I love the unloved child.
To be quite frank, this is the only time of year
To which I am by nature fully reconciled.
There is much good in it. I love it with sound reason,
Being aware of something special in this season.   40

6

How can this be explained? Autumn appeals to me
In the same way as a consumptive young girl might
Appeal to you. Condemned to death, poor creature, she
Fades uncomplainingly towards the gathering night.

Upon her pallid lips a playful smile you see.
The yawning grave is there, but still beyond her sight.
Her lovely face is delicately lilac-shot.
Today she is alive, tomorrow she is not.

7

Season of sadness! Now my eyes imbibe the splendour
With which you decorate the year as it grows old.   50
I love the countryside in all its fading grandeur,
The thinning of the woods, the purple and the gold,
Blown treetops whispering in voices soft and tender,
The leaden heavens where the rising mists have rolled,
The sudden sunbeams and the frost of early morning,
When greybeard Winter sends his first, long-distance warning.

8

In Autumn every year I come into full flower.
The thrilling Russian cold inspires me through and through.
I love my life again each day and every hour,
My appetite returns on time, and sleep does too,   60
My blood is up, my glad heart surges with new power,
Desire and joy are mine, I'm young, the world is new,
Fresh life wells up in me . . . Such is my constitution.
(If you'll forgive such a prosaical intrusion).

9

They bring my horse round. Mettlesome, he shakes his mane
And gallops off with me to range the open spaces.
The frozen valley now rings to a new refrain
Of clattering hoofs and cracking ice, as on he races.
But soon the short day fades and we are home again.
Too-long neglected, now how warm the fire-place is!   70
Flames flare, and fall. I read, and soon begin to ponder,
Letting my unrestrained imagination wander.

10

And I forget the world . . . The sweetness and the quiet
Lull all the feelings of my waking mind to rest.
Poetry comes to me; I am awakened by it.
Here is the lyric power, my spirit is possessed,

I tremble inwardly, magical sounds run riot,
My dreamed imaginings struggle to be expressed,
And visitors unseen swarm over me at last,
Figments of my fancy and people from my past.   80

11

Many the bold ideas that swim into my ken
And instantly meet rhymes to match them sweet and true.
The pen calls for my hand, the page demands the pen;
Poetry then pours forth in lines of every hue.
Thus may a galleon stand, becalmed and sleeping, when
Suddenly comes the call! At which the scrambling crew
Swarms up and down to spread the swelling canvas wide.
The giant sallies forth, cleaving the surging tide . . .

12

Where are we bound? . . .

(1833)

3 'I have outlived my aspirations'

I have outlived my aspirations,
I have outloved my every dream,
Suffering is my sole persuasion,
My heart feels only what has been.

Green was my garland – it has faded,   5
Blown by a destiny severe,
But I live on, alone and jaded,
Wondering if my end is near.

Defeated by the autumn frost,
With winter whistling down the heath,   10
On a bare branch, alone and lost,
I'm a forgotten, shivering leaf.

(1821)

4 Winter Evening

Darkness falling, stormy roaring,
Whipping winds and scurrying snow,
Baying beasts are howling for me,
Babies wailing – blow winds, blow,
Through the tattered rooftops flapping,
Rustling through the threadbare thatch,
Like a late-night traveller tapping,
Rattling at the window-latch.

Here inside your little cottage
All is sadness, all is gloom.   10
Dear old lady, you say nothing,
By the window of our room.
Are you weary of the windy
Blows and buffets that we feel,
Or the whirring of the spindle
And the whizzing of the wheel?

Here's to you, my dear old nanny,
Good companion of sad years.
Here's to grief – there isn't any!
Drink with me the cup that cheers.   20
Tell me tales again, old lady,
Sing to me again your rhymes,
Tales of tomtits and of maidens,
Tales of once upon a time.

Darkness falling, stormy roaring,
Whipping winds and scurrying snow,
Baying beasts are howling for me,
Babies wailing – blow winds, blow.
Here's to you, my dear old nanny,
Good companion of sad years.   30
Here's to grief – there isn't any!
Drink with me the cup that cheers.

(1825)

5 To my Nanny

True friend in all my times of trouble,
Dear frail companion, all alone
You languish in your woodland hovel,
Watching, waiting for my return.
You worry, peering through the glass;   5
Always on edge, you look and linger.
Your needles, as the minutes pass,
Stir slowly in your worn old fingers.
There are the lonely gates; your glances
Search past them down the long, black road.   10
Fretful, foreboding, ever-anxious,
You bear each hour a heavier load.
Oh, could this be . . . ?

                                        (1826)

6 Remembrance

When for us mortal men the noisy day is stilled,
    Hushing the city squares as they
Settle in limpid twilight languidly distilled,
    And sleep rewards the toil of day,
The hours unsleeping in interminable silence   5
    Draw out their long tormenting course;
In the blank night I feel with ever-sharper violence
    The serpent's sting of my remorse,
Imagination seethes, my mind is weighed with anguish,
    Swarming with dark ideas untold,   10
Before my eyes, remembrance speaks its silent language
    Disclosed on an uncoiling scroll;
Reading the ghastly story of my bygone days,
    I shudder, cursing, all-despising,

Burning with bitter tears – yet I shall not erase   15
   One line, however agonising.

(1828)

7   Foreboding

Once again the storm-clouds hover
In the silence over me;
Jealous Fate again hangs over,
Menacing my misery.
Shall I face my Fate, disdaining?
Shall I bear it and display
All the patience uncomplaining
That was mine in youth's proud day?

Tossed by stormy life and driven,
Careless of this storm I wait;   10
Maybe I shall find a haven
To protect me from my Fate . . .
But to part – my fear foretold it!
That dread hour we cannot flee.
Let me take your hand and hold it;
For the last time give it me.

Kind and quiet Angel, hear me:
Speak to me with soft goodbyes.
You have been so mournful. Near me
Let your sweet face fall or rise.   20
The remembrance of your caring
More than compensation pays
For the strength and pride and daring
And the hope of youthful days.

(1828)

Translation C. M. Bowra

8 'When I stroll down a busy street'

When I stroll down a busy street
Or linger in a crowded church
Or if wild youth and I should meet –
I let my idle dreams emerge.

I tell myself: the world keeps turning.
However many of us are here,
We're all bound for the vaults eternal,
And someone's hour is always near.

A lone oak-tree attracts my gaze;
I think: this patriarch sublime   10
Will long outlive these empty days,
As it outlived my father's time.

When I caress a little child
I think: Farewell, I've had my day.
You take my place, I'm reconciled –
Yours is to thrive, mine to decay.

I always say goodbye in thought
Each day, each year, and try to guess
Which day in which year will have brought
The anniversary of my death.   20

Where is my death? Where is my doom?
In battle? Far afield? At sea?
Or will perhaps some nearby combe
Encompass what remains of me?

Although the senseless human frame
Cares not at all where it should moulder,
I'd like to end up, all the same,
Near places that I once thought golden.

And at the entrance to my tomb
May young life frolic dissolutely,   30

And may impassive Nature bloom,
Shining with everlasting beauty.
                              (1829)

9   Elegy

The dead delights of frenzied younger days
Weigh on me like an alcoholic haze.
The aching sadness of my past endures
And, like good wine, gains body as it matures.
My future life is grim – without relief,   5
A surging swell of struggle, toil and grief.

And yet, my friends, I have no wish to die;
I want to suffer, live and wonder why.
I know I can expect, amid the torment,
Trouble and care, the rare delicious moment.   10
Sweet harmonies will fill me with delight
And I shall weep with joy for what I write.
And it may be that at my sad demise
A smile of love shall light in someone's eyes.
                              (1830)

10   'Take not away my wits, O God!'

Take not away my wits, O God!
Better the beggar's scrip and rod,
      To toil and not to eat!
It is not that I hold my mind
Of much account, or would not find
      The parting from it sweet.

If only they would set me free
To my own will, how glad I'd be

To seek the forest's shade.
In fiery frenzies I would sing, 10
And in my dreams' tumultuous swing
    All thoughts of self would fade.

I'd listen to the water's noise
And, brimming full of careless joys,
    Gaze on the empty sky;
Oh! then I should be free and strong,
A wind to course the plains along
    Or make the forests fly.

The curse is, if you lose your sense,
They shun you like a pestilence, 20
    And all your ways are tied.
They'll chain you to a madman's yoke,
And through the prison-bars provoke
    You like a beast inside.

No more in darkness shall I hear
The nightingale's voice ringing clear
    Or the black woodland's strains,
But only comrades' shrieks of fright,
And keepers' curses in the night,
    And screams, and clank of chains. 30

(1833)
Translation C. M. Bowra

11   'The time has come, dear friend'

The time has come, dear friend. My heart now longs for peace.
The days are flying by, and each hour as it flees
Subtracts a tiny bit of life. Though you and I
Make plans for life together – all too soon we die.
There is no happiness, but there is peace and freedom.

I have been dreaming of an enviable Eden:
Weary of slavery, long have I planned my flight
To a distant home of work and innocent delight.

                              (late poem, undated)

12 '. . . I visited again . . .'

                         . . . I visited again
That corner of the earth where once I spent,
In placid exile, two unheeded years.
A decade's gone since then – and in my life
There have been many changes – in myself,
Who from the general law am not exempt,
There have been changes, too – but here once more
The past envelops me, and suddenly
It seems that only yesterday I roamed
These groves.   10
                    Here stands the exile's cottage, where
I lived with my poor nurse. The good old woman
Has passed away – no longer do I hear
Through the thin wall her heavy tread as she
Goes on her busy rounds.
                              Here is the hill
Upon whose wooded crest I often sat
Unstirring, staring down upon the lake –
Recalling, as I looked, with melancholy,
Another shore, and other waves I knew . . .   20
Among the golden meadows, the green fields,
It stretches its blue breadth, the same still lake:
A fisherman across its lonely waters
Is rowing now, and dragging in his wake
A wretched net. Upon the sloping shores
Are scattered hamlets – and beyond them there
A mill squats crookedly – it scarcely stirs
Its wings in this soft wind . . .
                              Upon the edge

Of the ancestral acres, on the spot   30
Where the rough road, trenched by the heavy rains,
Begins its upward climb, three pine-trees rise –
One stands apart, and two are close together,
And I remember how, on moonlit nights,
When I rode past, their rustling greeted me
Like a familiar voice. I took that road,
I saw the pines before me once again.
They are the same, and on the ear the same
Familiar whisper breaks from shaken boughs,
But at the base, beside their aged roots   40
(Where I remembered only barrenness),
Has sprung a fair young grove, and I observe
A verdant family; the bushes crowd
Like children in their shadow. And apart,
Alone as ever, their glum comrade stands,
Like an old bachelor, about whose feet
There stretches only bareness as before.
I hail you, race of youthful newcomers!
I shall not witness your maturity,
When you shall have outgrown my ancient friends,   50
And with your shoulders hide their very heads
From passers-by. But let my grandson hear
Your wordless greeting when, as he returns,
Content, light-hearted, from a talk with friends,
He too rides past you in the dark of night,
And thinks, perhaps, of me.

                                              (1835)
                                  Translation B. Deutsch

13   A Zephyr flies

A zephyr flies
Through evening skies.
And roars,
And pours,
Guadalquivir.   5

Lo, the golden moon is shining:
Hark, a soft guitar's refrain . . .
On her balcony reclining,
See, there leans a maid of Spain.
   A zephyr flies   10
   Through evening skies.
   And roars,
   And pours,
   Guadalquivir.
Shed thy cloak, thy form displaying,   15
Like a radiant dawn, fair maid:
Let thy wondrous foot come straying,
Through the iron-wrought balustrade.
   A zephyr flies
   Through evening skies.   20
   And roars,
   And pours,
   Guadalquivir.

(1824)
Translation P. Selver

14   The Don

Through open fields, across the plain,
I see him yonder, streaming on!
From all your distant sons, again
I give you greetings, shining Don.

O quiet Don, each river knows   5
That you their famous brother are;
Araxes greets you as he flows,
As does Euphrates from afar.

By cruel foes no longer chased
The horses of the Don draw nigh,   10

Scenting their home at last, and taste
The welcome streams of Arpachai.

Stand ready, holy Don, for there
They come, brave Cossacks, born your own!
Once more the sparkling wine prepare   15
Coming from vineyards you have grown.

                                        (1829)

15   Winter Morning

Miraculous morning! Frost and sun!
But you, delightful friend, sleep on.
'Tis time for beauty to bestir.
Open your soft and drowsy eyes
To greet the Dawn in northern skies,
A northern star to welcome her.

Last night, remember, a wind blew;
In the rough sky a thick mist grew,
And the moon, like a pallid smear,
Was yellow through the gloomy cloud.   10
In melancholy you sat bowed.
But now, look through the window there!

Snow underneath the clear blue skies
Glitters in sunlight as it lies;
A gorgeous coverlet it glows.
Black though the wood's transparent screen,
The fir-trees through the frost are green;
The streams are bright beneath the floes.

Now every room with amber light
Is blazing. Crackling with delight   20
The stove bursts into heat and flares.
It's good to sit and dream today;

But won't you tell them get the sleigh
And harness up the chestnut mares?

Across the slippery morning snow,
My sweet companion, we shall go
And let the restless horses race;
We'll visit lonely fields of grass,
Woods where in summer none can pass,
And river-bank, my most loved place.

(1829)
Translation C. M. Bowra

16   The Caucasus

I stand above the Caucasus, where lies
    By the cold torrent's edge the waste of snow;
Motionless hovers, level with my eyes,
    An eagle risen from a peak below.
Here is the birthplace of the streams, and here
The first dread motions of the avalanche stir.

Below me pass the clouds, serenely fair;
    Through them the falling waters ever sound;
Far down, the shoulders of the rocks are bare,
    Grey scrub and meagre mosses clothe the ground;   10
And lower yet, filled with the sound of birds,
Are leafy forests and the deer in herds.

Next, roofs that nestle in the mountain sides,
    And sheep that crop the grass by torrent streams;
Down to the happy vale the shepherd strides,
    Past shadowed banks the swift Aragva gleams,
Whilst in the gorge the robber tribesmen wait
Where sweeps the Terek in triumphant spate.

Like a young beast of prey the river roars,
    Wild for its food through iron bars and locks;   20

With frustrate anger he assaults the shores
    And with his hungry current licks the rocks,
In vain; no comfort's here, no food for him;
The unhearing gorge confines him, hard and grim.

Thus by our edicts an impetuous nation
    Of wild free tribesmen lies oppressed and bound,
And silent Caucasus with indignation
    Seethes as the alien forces hem him round . . .

                  (1829)
           Translation F. Cornford

17 The Avalanche

Beaten by jagged rocks to steam,
Before me pours the boiling stream;
Above my head the eagles scream,
    The pine-wood speaks,
And through the mist there faintly gleam
    The mountain-peaks.

From where the snow-clad summits soar
An avalanche in days of yore
Thundering down with mighty roar
    The channel filled
Through which the river Terek tore
    Impetuous-willed.

Its waters lake-wise spread about,
A moment Terek stilled its shout,
Until the last waves' raging rout
    Burst through the snow
And, filled with fury, battered out
    A path below.

And there the snow for many a day
In huge, unmelting masses lay;

10

20

Beneath, fierce Terek bored a way
　　That naught could halt
And spattered with a noisy spray
　　The icy vault.

And o'er the snow a wide road led:
There oxen plodded, horses sped,
Leading his camel by the head
　　The merchant passed,
Where rushes now through caverns dread
　　The wind's chill blast.

(1829)
Translation W. Morrison

18　Demons

Storm-clouds whirl and storm-clouds scurry;
From behind them pale moonlight
Flickers where the snowflakes hurry.
Dark the sky, and dark the night.
On and on the sleigh still bears me;
Ding-ding-ding the small bell's sound.
Though I would not, something scares me
In the unknown plains around.

'Go on, driver!' . . . 'I can't go, sir.
The horses find it hard to pull,　　　　　　　　　　10
And my eyes are blind with snow, sir;
Drifts have blocked the whole road full.
Strike me, but I search it vainly!
We are lost! What's to be done?
'Tis a devil leads us, plainly, –
From the road would have us gone.

'Over there – Look! See him playing,
Blowing, spitting in my eye.
In the ditch he sends a-straying

This poor horse, and makes him shy.   20
Like a milestone weird he glimmered;
There in front he stood upright;
Like a tiny spark he shimmered,
Vanished in the empty night.'

Storm-clouds whirl and storm-clouds scurry;
From behind them pale moonlight
Flickers where the snowflakes hurry.
Dark the sky, and dark the night.
Tired, we have no strength for wheeling.
Bell stops jingling, suddenly.   30
Halt . . . 'What is the plain concealing?
Who can tell you? Wolf or tree?'

Blizzard angry, blizzard crying,
Horses start and snort in fear.
Farther on again he's flying;
In the night his eyes burn clear.
Horses now go forward, straining;
Ding-ding-ding, the small bell's sound.
There I see the phantoms gaining
In the plain that whitens round.   40

Fiends past number, formless, curling
In the play of dim moonlight –
Demons manifold are whirling,
Like November leaves in flight!
Crowds of them! Where do they hurry?
Why this song in mournful pitch?
Is it goblins that they bury?
Make they marriage for a witch?

Storm-clouds whirl and storm-clouds scurry;
From behind them pale moonlight   50
Flickers where the snowflakes hurry.
Dark the sky, and dark the night.
Onward run the devils, sailing

In the measureless inane,
And their howls and mournful wailing
Nearly tear my heart in twain.

(1830)
Translation C. M. Bowra

19   The Cloud

Last cloud of a storm that is scattered and over,
Alone in the skies of bright azure you hover,
Alone with sad shadows you float on your way,
Alone you throw gloom on the joy of the day.

By you all the heaven was lately confounded,   5
You were with the hideous lightning surrounded,
You rang the mysterious thunderclap out,
You rained on the earth that was thirsting in drought.

Enough, and begone! 'Tis no time for your power.
The earth is refreshed now, and finished the shower;   10
And the breeze that caresses the leaves as it flies
Will chase you away from the quieted skies.

(1835)
Translation C. M. Bowra

20   The Prophet

My spirit failed; lost and tormented,
I roamed the wilderness, wherein
Facing a crossroads I encountered
A glorious six-winged seraphim.

He touched me, dreamlike, feather-fingered,
Upon my very eyes he lingered;
They shone, like a shocked eaglet's, wide,
Prophetically revivified;
He touched my ears, into them pouring
A ringing and a mighty roaring; 10
I heard the shuddering heavens speak
And angels soaring in the vault
And sea-beasts squirming in the salt
And in the valleys vines that creaked.
He touched my mouth and from it wrung
My sinfully backbiting tongue,
Full of deceit, and he inserted
With fingers dripping yet with blood
Into my palsied mouth for good
The sting and wisdom of a serpent, 20
And with his sword he clove my breast
And tore out from the bleeding hole
My throbbing heart, and into it pressed
Another heart of burning coal.

I lay like death where I had trod
And hearkened to the voice of God:

Prophet, arise and follow me,
Seeing and hearing, saith the Lord.
Go forth upon the land and sea
And burn hearts with the living Word.

(1826)

21 The Poet

Until the poet hears Apollo's
Call to the hallowed sacrifice,
The petty cares of life he follows,
And sunk in them his spirit lies.
His holy lyre remains unsounded; 5

His spirit sleeps in numbing rest,
By an unworthy world surrounded,
Himself perhaps unworthiest.

But once his ear, attentive, shakes
When the god-given word is stirring,   10
The poet's soul, its pinions whirring,
Is like an eagle that awakes.
Then wearied of all worldly playing,
He shuns the babble of the crowd;
The people's idol disobeying,   15
His haughty head remains unbowed.
He runs away, and wildly, proudly,
Comes full of riot, full of sound,
Where empty waters wash around
The shores and woods that echo loudly.
                              (1826)
                    Translation C. M. Bowra

22   To the Poet

When all acclaim you, Poet, pay no heed!
The sound of clapping soon will die; instead
You'll hear fools judge, the cold crowd mock your deed:
Be calm, austere, with proudly-lifted head.

You're king, so dwell alone. Your free path tread   5
Wherever your free mind your steps may lead;
Perfect the fruits your secret thoughts have bred,
And for your high achievement ask no meed.

It is within. You are your highest judge;
Sooner than other critics, praise you grudge;   10
Can you your own sharp criticism meet?

You can? Then let the mob besmirch your name,
Spit on the altar that enshrines your flame.

In childish horse-play shake your tripod's feet.

(1830)

Translation W. Morrison

23   *Exegi Monumentum*

I have my monument, not built by human hands.
Well-worn shall be the way to it that men shall follow.
Indomitable it has raised its head, which stands
   Higher than Alexander's Column.

Not all of me shall die, for in my lyric strains   5
My spirit shall endure – the grave shall not destroy it.
I shall be famous still while ever there remains
   Under the moon a single poet.

Word of me shall go out through all the lands of Rus,
Where each and every people shall pronounce my name –   10
That grandson of the Slavs, the Finn, the wild Tungus
   And the Kalmyk out on the plain.

Long shall the people love my name, and for good reason:
That I was one who roused kind feelings by my verses,
That in a cruel age I sang the cause of freedom   15
   And for the fallen called for mercy.

Hearken, O Muse, to what is ordered in God's name:
Ignore all calumny and ask no crown or jewels,
Receive with equanimity both praise and blame.
   Do this – and have no truck with fools.

(1836)

24 The Singer

Ah, did you hear, beyond the groves at night,
  The singer who of love and grief doth sing?
When fields were mute, the sun's bright dawn awaiting,
  The sound of pipes, so sad and yet so light, –
    Ah, did you hear?   5

Ah, did you meet in darkened woods by chance,
  The singer who of love and grief doth sing?
His tears did you behold, or saw him smiling,
  Or all the grief that shimmers in his glance, –
    Ah, did you meet?   10

Ah, did you sigh to hear that quiet voice, –
  The singer who of love and grief doth sing?
When in the woods you met him wandering,
  When on you fell his eyes that never will rejoice, –
    Ah, did you sigh?

                                            (1816)
                                    Translation anon

25 'The rain-quenched day has died'

The rain-quenched day has died; across the rain-drenched sky
The mists of night unroll their coverings of lead;
Just like a ghost, from where the pines their shadows spread
    A misty moon creeps high . . .
All, all around me fills my aching soul with tears.   5
There, far away, the moon in radiance appears;
The air is balmy there with the warm breath of eve;
There intertwining waves a precious fabric weave;
    There skies of azure soar . . .
It is the hour! Now down the shadowed hill she goes   10
To where the sleepy sea beats sighing on the shore;
    There, in the rocks' most secret core,

In solitude she sits, enfolded in her woes . . .
Alone . . . There's none to weep before her, or lament;
None to embrace her knees, his heart with rapture rent;   15
Alone . . . She cannot yield to any lips' delight
Her shoulders, her wet lips, her breasts of snowy white

. . . .

. . . .

. . . .   20

None is there to deserve that love from heaven sent.
Not so? You are alone, and weeping . . . I'm content.

. . . .

But if . . .

(1824)
Translation W. Morrison

26 Gypsy girl's song

(*from* The Gypsies)

Grey old man, savage man,
Slice me up, burn me dead.
I am proud. Not the knife,
Not the fire shall I dread.

Naught for you but disdain,   5
Naught but loathing, have I;
For I love someone else,
And for love I shall die.

Slice me up, burn me dead.
Nothing shall I betray.   10
Grey old man, savage man,
Who he is I'll not say!

Summer burns not so hot,
Not so bright spring as he.

He is young, he is brave.   15
What a love his for me!

How I gave him my love
In the still hours of night!
How we laughed, both of us,
At your hair turning white!
                              (1824)
               Translation C. M. Bowra

27   A Confession

I love you – love you, even as I
Rage at myself for this obsession,
And as I make my shamed confession,
Despairing at your feet I lie.
I know, I know – it ill becomes me,
I am too old, time to be wise . . .
But how? . . . This love – it overcomes me,
A sickness this in passion's guise.
When you are near I'm filled with sadness,
When far, I yawn, for life's a bore.   10
I must pour out this love, this madness,
There's nothing that I long for more!
When your skirts rustle, when, my angel,
Your girlish voice I hear, when your
Light step sounds in the parlour – strangely,
I turn confused, perturbed, unsure.
You frown – and I'm in pain, I languish;
You smile – and joy defeats distress;
My one reward for a day's anguish
Comes when your pale hand, love, I kiss.   20
When you sit bent over your sewing,
Your eyes cast down and fine curls blowing
About your face, with tenderness
I childlike watch, my heart o'erflowing
With love, in my gaze a caress.

Shall I my jealousy and yearning
Describe, my bitterness and woe
When by yourself on some bleak morning
Off on a distant walk you go,
Or with another spend the evening   30
And, with him near, the piano play,
Or for Opóchka leave, or, grieving,
Weep and in silence pass the day? . . .
Alina! Pray relent, have mercy!
I dare not ask for love – with all
My many sins, both great and small,
I am perhaps of love unworthy! . . .
But if you feigned love, if you would
Pretend, you'd easily deceive me,
For happily would I, believe me,   40
Deceive myself if but I could!

(1824)
Translation I. Zheleznova

28   To Anna Kern

I still remember all the wonder,
The glorious thrill of meeting you,
The momentary spell of splendour,
Spirit of beauty pure and true.

When sadness came upon me, endless,
In vain society's direst days,
I heard your voice, your accents tender,
And dreamt of heaven in your face.

Years passed, with stormy days diffusing
My young dreams into empty space,   10
And I forgot your voice's music
And heaven's beauty in your face.

Then far from home in exile, chastened,
I watched the weary days go by.
No tears for me, no inspiration,
No sense of God, no love, no life.

You came again. My soul remembered
The glorious thrill of meeting you,
The momentary spell of splendour,
Spirit of beauty pure and true.   20

Now once again my heart is racing,
Proclaiming the renewal of
My former tears, my inspiration,
My sense of God, and life, and love.
(1825)

29 'Beneath the blue skies of her homeland'

Beneath the blue skies of her homeland, she
   Fell languishing and withering,
Faded at last; and her young shade, maybe,
   Already touched me with its wing.
Between us is a line impassable.   5
   In vain I tried to wake my sense.
I heard indifferent lips of her death tell;
   I listened with indifference.
So this is she I loved with soul afire,
   With spirit in so dolorous stress,   10
With such a sweet and languishing desire,
   Such suffering, such foolishness.
Where are love's torments? In my heart, alack,
   For that poor shadow confident,
For sweet remembered days that come not back,   15
   I find no tear and no lament.
(1826)
Translation C. M. Bowra

30   The Talisman

Once, far away, where strong seas rise
Surging to beat on barren cliffs,
Where moonlight shines from warmer skies
And scents across the evening drift,
Where with his wives in endless bliss
Lives the devout Mohammedan,
A sorceress with a loving kiss
Gave me a gift – a talisman.

She said, with kisses and caresses,
'Never give up my talisman.   10
A secret magic it possesses,
Holding my love within its span.
If sickness, storms or death contrive
Against you, dear, please understand
That in such days you shall derive
No solace from my talisman.

It will not bring great wealth to you.
Expect no Eastern treasures of it,
Nor will it help you to subdue
The faithful followers of the prophet.   20
Home to the arms of friends who need you,
From the sad south across the land
To the good north it cannot speed you,
The magic of my talisman.

But if some fickle woman might
Suddenly threaten to beguile you,
If woman's lips in the dark night
With loveless kisses would defile you –
My darling, in the face of wrong.
Of fresh wounds by a woman's hand,   30
Of faithlessness and loss, be strong!
Magical is my talisman.

(1827)

31   'The mournful melodies that fall'

The mournful melodies that fall
From Georgian lips, maid, sing no more!
Those songs too hauntingly recall
Another life, a distant shore.

Each sad refrain, each sombre tune   5
Sung, fair one, with your wonted grace,
Recalls the steppe, the night, the moon,
A far-off maiden's misty face.

I gaze upon you, and forget
That lovely shade in sorrow set;   10
But when you sing, before my eyes
Her half-remembered features rise.

The mournful melodies that fall
From Georgian lips, maid, sing no more;
For they too hauntingly recall   15
Another life, a distant shore.

(1828)
Translation W. Morrison

32   The Flower

I found a flower forlorn and sere,
No longer scented, in a book,
And by a curious idea
My wondering spirit has been struck.

Where, when, in what spring did it grow?   5
How old was it? Who picked it, who?
Some stranger, or someone I know?
And what was it supposed to do?

To mark a meeting of twin souls
Or some dire parting of the ways?   10
Or just a solitary stroll
Through quiet fields or woodland shade?

And is he still alive? Is she?
Where are they now, where is their nook?
Or have they faded finally   15
Like this lost flower in the book?

(1828)

33   'The shadows of the night lie on the Georgian hills'

The shadows of the night lie on the Georgian hills,
    And there is the Aragva calling.
I'm sad, and not sad, with a radiant sorrow filled,
    A sorrow made of you, my darling,
Of you, and you alone . . . My weariness of soul
    Cannot be moved. With memories of you
My heart renews its love and burns beyond control.
    It has no choice – it has to love you.

(1829)

34   *from* Hafiz

Camp on the Euphrates

Lovely youth, when war-drums rattle
Be not ravished: seal your ears;
Do not leap into the battle
With the crowd of mountaineers.
Well I know that death will shun you,   5

And that where the sabres fly
Azrael will look upon you,
Note your beauty, and pass by!
But the war will be unsparing:
You, I fear, must suffer harm –   10
Lose your timid grace of bearing,
Lose your shy and languid charm.

(1829)

Translation B. Deutsch

35 'Oh, I have loved you'

Oh, I have loved you, and perhaps my spirit
Still harbours a warm glow of love today.
But God forbid that you be burdened with it;
I would not sadden you in any way.

I loved you in a wordless, hopeless fashion,   5
Sometimes in jealous rage, sometimes struck dumb.
I loved you with a deep and tender passion.
May you be loved like this in years to come.

(1829)

36 'What is my name to you?'

What is my name to you? . . . 'Twill die
As does the melancholy murmur
Of distant waves or, in the summer,
The forest's hushed nocturnal sigh.

Found on a fading album page,   5
Dim will it seem and enigmatic,

Like words traced on a tomb, a relic
Of some long dead and vanished age.

What's in my name? . . . Long since forgot,
Erased by new, tempestuous passion,   10
Of tenderness 'twill leave you not
The lingering and sweet impression.

But in an hour of agony,
Pray, speak it, and recall my image,
And say, 'He still remembers me,   15
His heart alone still pays me homage.'
                                        (1830)
                          Translation I. Zheleznova

37 'Towards the shores
of your far homeland'

Towards the shores of your far homeland
From alien strands your footsteps led;
When we our last sad kisses mingled
Tears unforgettable I shed.
The movements of my chilly fingers
Begged you a moment yet to dwell;
My voice, that shook with sorrow, bade you
Lengthen the anguish of farewell.

But from my lips' impassioned pleading
Your lips despairingly you tore;   10
Departing, from my sombre exile
You called me to another shore.
You said: When we're again together
Beneath a sky for ever bright,
Our lips beneath the shade of olives
Once more, my sweetheart, we'll unite.

But there, alas, where purest azure
Fills the wide vaulting of the sky,
Where 'neath the rocks the waters slumber
Sunk in your last long sleep you lie.   20
Your beauty, all the pains you suffered,
Have vanished with you in the tomb –
With you, the promised kiss of union . . .
I wait; that kiss is still to come! . . .

(1830)
Translation W. Morrison

38   'No, not for me the stormiest pleasures of the senses'

No, not for me the stormiest pleasures of the senses,
Voluptuous enjoyment, overwhelming frenzies,
No, not the groans of some Bacchante, or her cries
When, squirming like a snake, in my embrace she lies,
Hurrying me along, eager to know what bliss is,   5
And shuddering to her crisis in a storm of kisses.
No, you're much lovelier than this, my gentle lamb.
How agonisingly happy with you I am
When you have said you won't and now you say you will,
Only to yield yourself with no delight or thrill,   10
Cold to my protestations and exuberance,
Restrained in sympathy and lukewarm in response,
Until I feel you melt, in your reluctant fashion,
Coming to me at last and sharing in my passion.

(1830)

39 'When I reach over to enfold you'

When I reach over to enfold you,
Encompassing your slender form
And ever breathing as I hold you
Transports of love to keep you warm,
You slither from me silently   5
With such a lithe and lively rhythm;
Then, darling, you respond to me
With a sharp smile of scepticism.
Determined never to forget
A sad tradition of betrayal,   10
Unsympathetic and upset,
You scarcely heed my lover's tale . . .
I curse the ventures mean and shady
Of distant days when youth ran riot,
Waiting in gardens for young ladies,   15
All anxious in the evening quiet.
I curse love's whispering in the ears,
The magic melody of verse,
The easy girls, and, what is worse,
Their late misgivings and their tears . . .

(1830)

40 'I thought my heart had long forgotten'

I thought my heart had long forgotten
How easy it is to suffer pain.
I used to say, 'The past is nothing.
It cannot ever come again.'

Sadness and joy were gone for ever,
Like dreams abandoned absolutely,
But here they are again, aquiver
Before unconquerable beauty.

(1835)

41 To Chaadayev

Not long we basked in the illusion
Of love, of hope, of quiet fame;
Like morning mists, a dream's delusion,
Youth's pastimes vanished as they came.
But still, with strong desires burning,
Beneath oppression's fateful hand,
The summons of the fatherland
We are impatiently discerning;
In hope, in torment, we are turning
Towards freedom, waiting her command –　　　　10
Thus anguished do young lovers stand
Who wait the promised tryst with yearning.
While freedom kindles us, my friend,
While honour calls us and we hear it,
Come: to our country let us tend
The noble promptings of the spirit.
Comrade, believe: joy's star will leap
Upon our sight, a radiant token;
Russia will rouse from her long sleep;
And where autocracy lies, broken,　　　　20
Our names shall yet be graven deep.

(1818)
Translation B. Deutsch

42 Grapes

I shall not rue the fading lustre
Of roses in the short-lived spring,
My love is for the ripening clusters
Of grapes upon the slopes, which bring
To my rich valley a new splendour
Across the golden autumn land,
Growing transparent, long and slender,
Like fingers on a young girl's hand.

(1820)

43   The Waggon of Life

Though creaking sometimes with the load,
Life's running waggon scarcely rocks.
Grey Time conducts us down the road;
This driver never leaves the box.

We climb upon the boards at dawn   5
Full of wild devilment and crowing;
Spurning the languid life with scorn,
We cry, 'Go on, get fucking going!'

But by midday we've lost that boldness,
Feeling the waggon shake and judder.   10
Dread are the heights and dizzy gorges.
We cry, 'Slow down, you silly bugger!'

On goes the waggon round the bend.
By evening well we know the rhythm.
Nodding, we ride to our journey's end   15
Time's waggon ever-onward driven.

                              (1823)

44   'Life may not fulfil its promise'

Life may not fulfil its promise,
Be not angry or dismayed,
Do not dread the dismal days –
Days of happiness are coming.

Love is in the future tense,   5
Not the unsatisfying present.
All that happens passes hence;
That which passes shall be pleasant.

                              (1825)

45 Bacchanal Song

Why, revelry's voice, are you still?
Ring out, songs of Bacchus, our patron!
Long life to you, maiden and matron,
Ye fair ones who gave of your love with a will!
  Drink, friend, drink with gusto and relish!
      As I do in mine,
      In your glass of wine
  Fling lightly the ring that you cherish!
Come, let's clink our glasses and high let us raise them!
Hail, muses! Hail, reason! In song let us praise them!   10
  Thou, bright sun of genius, shine on!
  Like this ancient lamp that grows dimmer
  And fades with the coming of dawn,
So false wisdom pales at the first tiny glimmer
  Of true wisdom's ne'er-fading light . . .   15
Live, radiant day! Perish, darkness and night!

                    (1825)
           Translation I. Zheleznova

46 Three Springs

On life's wide wilderness of endless sadness
Three springs mysteriously have bubbled forth.
The spring of youth is one of speed and challenge;
It seethes and glitters, gurgling through the earth.
The second spring, Castalian, original,   5
Feeds inspiration to those cast apart.
The last spring is the cold spring of oblivion –
There is no sweeter balm to soothe the heart.

                    (1827)

47   'Gift of life so useless'

Gift of life so useless, why
Did you have to come to me?
Why were you condemned to die
By some secret destiny?

From the void why did I start,   5
Summoned by a hostile force,
Putting passion in my heart,
In my mind doubt and remorse?

There's no goal, I shall not strive;
Blank my mind, my heart is empty.   10
I am weary that my life
Murmurs on inconsequently.

(1828)

48   The Upas Tree

In parched and barren desert land
Where blazing sunshine sears the earth
The Upas Tree, a grim guard, stands
Alone in all the universe.

Nature one day on that dry plain
Begot it in a surge of wrath
Piercing the dead green leaves to stain
Its boughs and roots with a poisoned broth.

Now poison oozes through the bark,
Melting at high noon, to become   10
Hard and stiff in the evening dark,
Glassy coagulated gum.

No bird, no tiger dare approach.
Only black whirlwinds on occasion
Visit this pestilential growth
And speed off with their vile contagion.

And if a roving cloud should chance
To moisten its thick leafy strands
From every newly-poisoned branch
Dark poison laves the burning sands.   20

But one man sent another man
To the Upas Tree, by order stern.
Obediently away he ran
And with the poison soon returned.

He brought the deadly gum. The bough
And its fine foliage were withered.
Suddenly down his pallid brow
Cold streams of perspiration slithered.

He brought the gum and lay down, weak,
On the tent matting. Moments later   30
The poor slave perished at the feet
Of the implacable dictator,

Who soaked his slavish arrow-heads
With poison sure to overwhelm,
Disseminating by them death
To humankind in every realm.

         (1828)

49 Madonna

Not by old masters, rich on crowded walls,
My house I ever sought to ornament,
That gaping guests might marvel while they leant
To connoisseurs with condescending drawls.
Amidst slow labours, far from garish halls,   5
Before one picture I would fain have spent
Eternity: where the calm canvas thralls
As though the Virgin and the Saviour bent
From regnant clouds, the Glorious and the Wise,
The meek and hallowed, with unearthly eyes,   10
Beneath the palm of Zion, these alone . . .
My wish is granted: God has shown thy face
To me; here, my Madonna, thou shalt throne:
Most pure exemplar of the purest grace.

(1830)
Translation B. Deutsch

50   Verses composed during a sleepless night

I can't sleep, though it is dark,
Lights are out, the lucky slumber.
Moments of my night are numbered
By a monotonous tick-tock,
Fate foretold in women's chatter,   5
In the sleepy night a flutter,
Life itself, a little mouse,
Scurrying. Dark thoughts are roused –
Where's your meaning, weary whisper?
Do you chide the lazy listener   10
For a lost day petering out?

How can I begin to suit you?
Call to me, or tell my future.
Let me understand you! Oh,
Is there sense? I need to know.
(1830)

51   The Beauty

All harmony, all marvel, she,
Above the world and passionless:
She rests serene shamefastedly
In her triumphant loveliness;
She looks around her left and right: 5
She has no rival and no peer:
The beauties of our pallid sphere
Have vanished in her blinding light.

Bound for whatever be your goal,
Though to a lover's tryst you speed,   10
However precious in your soul
A day-dream you may hide and feed;
Yet, meeting her, unwillingly
You of a sudden dazed and mute
Shall halt devoutly to salute   15
Her beauty and her sanctity.
(1832)

Translation Hon. M. Baring

52 'Hermits and blameless women full of Grace'

Hermits and blameless women full of Grace,
To raise the heart into celestial space,
In storm and strife below to strengthen it,
A host of holy orisons have writ;
But one of all the multitudinous host   5
Of orison and praise has moved me most,
A prayer repeated by the priest in Lent,
In the dark days of fasting and lament:
Upon my lips more often it will dwell –
And breathe on the faint soul a vital spell: 10
'O Ruler of my days! Ward off from me
The evil angel of despondency
And sloth; and let not from my lips be heard
The sharp repeating of the idle word;
Save me from lust, that snake which lives within;   15
And let me not be blind to my own sin,
Blind to my brother's trespass let me,
Quicken the spirit of consent in me,
Of love, long-suffering and of chastity.'

                                        (1836)
                        Translation Hon. M. Baring

53 'When, lost in thought, I roam'

When, lost in thought, I roam beyond the city's bounds
And find myself within the public burial-grounds,
The fashionable tombs behind the railing squatting,
Where the great capital's uncounted dead are rotting,
All huddled in a swamp, a crowding, teeming horde,
Like greedy guests that swarm about a beggar's board;
Officials' sepulchers, and merchants', too, all fizzles:
The clumsy products of inexpert, vulgar chisels,

Inscribed in prose and verse with virtues, service, rank,
Outlandish ornaments displayed on either flank;   10
A widow's fond lament for an old cuckold coffined;
The urns screwed from their posts by thieves; the earth that's
     softened
And slippery, where graves are gaping dark and wide
To welcome tenants who next day will move inside –
All this brings troubled thoughts; I feel my spirits fail me
As I survey the scene, and evil blues assail me.
One wants to spit and run!
                         But what calm pleasure lies –
When rural autumn sheds its peace from evening skies –
In seeing the churchyard, where, solemnly reposing
Among their ancestors, the country dead are dozing!   20
There, unadorned, the graves have ample elbow-room;
At midnight no pale thief creeps forth to rob the tomb;
The peasant sighs and says a prayer as he passes
The time-worn stones o'ergrown with yellowed moss
     and grasses;
No noseless angels soar, no blowsy Graces here,
No petty pyramids or idle urns appear;
But a broad oak above these dignified graves brooding
Bestirs its boughs in music . . .

                                         (1836)
                         Translation B. Deutsch

54   'Deep down in your Siberian mine'

Deep down in your Siberian mine
Stand steadfast in enduring pride.
Your grievous toil is not in vain,
Nor are your noble thoughts denied.

Hope shall sustain her sister, sorrow,   5
Through all the dark infernal night,
Bringing new courage and delight,
The sureness of a new tomorrow.

In love and friendship you abound,
Unlocking doors in dungeons foreign 10
Where, ringing through your convicts' warren,
My liberating voice shall sound.

Away the bars, the shackling chain,
Down with the prison and the captor,
Freedom waits at the gate with rapture, 15
Brothers shall hand you swords again.

(1827)

55 Arion

Many were crowded on the craft.
Some of us stretched the sail, while others
Toiled with the plunging oars like brothers,
Cleaving the deep. Our helmsman aft
Set the course, deftly steering us 5
Upon our silent, laden ship.
I sang; my easy strains had gripped
The crew. But then the waves were whipped
By a sudden swooping, swingeing gust . . .
Pilot and crew sank in an instant, 10
But I lived on, their solemn minstrel.
On to the foreshore I was dragged
Where I lay down my weary limbs
And there resumed my former hymns,
Drying my clothes beneath a crag.

(1827)

56   from *Boris Godunov*: Pimen's Monologue

1603. A Cell in the Monastery of the Miracle. Night.

Pimen (*writing under a lamp*)

One record more remains, the last of all,
And then this chronicle of mine is finished,
The duty is fulfilled which God has laid
On me, a sinner. Of these many years
The Lord has made me witness not in vain
And taught me the intelligence of books.
In days to come some never-tiring monk
Will come across my nameless, patient work.
As I have done, so will he light his lamp
And shake the dust of ages from these words   10
And then transcribe the veritable records.
Thus shall the future sons of Orthodoxy
Learn the old fortunes of their native land
And call to mind their great tsars, well-remembered
For all their labours, glories and good works –
Whilst for their sins and for their darkest deeds
Before the Saviour making supplication.
    Now in old age I live my life anew
As bygone years proceed before my eyes.
Are they so long-departed, filled with action   20
And agitated like the ocean seas?
Now they remain unspeaking and at peace.
Few faces now my memory retains,
Few words survive to call upon my ear.
The rest has gone irrevocably by . . .
But day is near, my lamp is burning low.
One record more remains, the last of all . . . (*he writes*)

(1825)

57 from *Yevgeny Onegin*

These are the concluding stanzas of Pushkin's novel in verse
(Chapter 8, Stanzas 33–51)

*Some three years before, the disenchanted Onegin inherited a country
estate and became involved with several neighbouring families. Through
a young acquaintance, Vladimir Lensky, he met the Larins; Tatyana
Larina wrote a letter to him, offering her love, which he rejected.
Following a quarrel Onegin killed Lensky in a duel. Now in the final
chapter of the novel he returns to St Petersburg, where Tatyana has
become a high-society hostess. It is his turn to suffer. He offers his love to
her, also in a letter, and waits anxiously for a reply.*

33
– No answer. Now behold him sending
Another letter – and one more.
No answer! Next, he is attending
A party; scarce within the door,
And – there is she . . . and how severely
She looks! She disregards him merely,
And speaks not. Ugh! he feels a cold,
Like January's, her enfold!
Those stubborn lips – what indignation
Are they not seeking to restrain?
He gazes fixedly – in vain
Seeks sympathy, or perturbation,
Or marks of tears . . . none, none! that face
Of naught but anger bears the trace.

34
Perhaps she fears herself in secret,
Lest to her husband she expose
– Or to the world – that slip, that weakness,
And all that my Onegin knows.
And now he drives away, despairing;
And, ever at his madness swearing,
Into its lowest deep is hurled,
And, once again, abjures the world;

Then, in his silent room, renewing
The past, remembers how the spleen
Through that same noisy world had been
Relentlessly his tracks pursuing,
And straightway by the collar took
And shut him in his gloomy nook.

35

Once more, he started random reading:
– Manzoni, Gibbon, and Rousseau;
Through Herder and De Staël proceeding,
And through Bichat, Chamfort, Tissot;
Read Bayle the sceptic's lucubrations,
Read all of Fontenelle's creations;
Some Russian author (please select!),
And nothing printed would reject:
Journals, or almanacks, repeating
Instructive precepts. Though they scold
Me now, it was not so of old;
They used to give me friendly greeting
With madrigals of praise; so, then,
È *sempre bene*, gentlemen!

36

His wrapt attention, though, was hollow;
His thoughts ranged far, beyond control.
Fanciful dreams, desire and sorrow
Were huddled deep within his soul.
Whilst on the printed lines he brooded,
Quite other lines and words intruded
Upon his spiritual eye,
And these engrossed him utterly:–
The dark mysterious traditions
Of days when hearts were warm and true;
And rumours, dreams without a clue,
And threatenings, and premonitions;
Gay, silly folktales, slow to end;
– Or letters, by a maiden penned.

37

A drowsy stupor now enfolds him;
Feeling and thought he disregards.
Mistress Imagination holds him,
Dealing her motley *faro* cards.
On soft snow – useless to deny it –
A young man lies, all still and quiet,
As if he has just gone to bed.
A voice is heard: 'That's it. He's dead.'
He sees old foes, calumniators,
Cowards, malignant; many a sworn
Comrade, whom now he holds in scorn;
A troop of women, young – all traitors!
Next, at a rural window, he
Beholds her sit – 'tis always She! . . .

38

Into this dreamy habit falling,
He very nearly lost his wit,
Or went the poet's way – a calling
So dire, don't even think of it!
And so, indeed, by power magnetic,
The nice machinery poetic
Of Russian verse he all but caught,
– This foolish fellow, whom I taught.
And, in a poet, how becoming
His air, when lost in his alcove,
He sat before the blazing stove,
And there, while *Benedetta* humming
Or purring *Idol mio* – *The News*
Dropt in the fire – or else his shoes.

39

The days sped by. Ere one could know it,
Winter dissolved in warmth. Though sad,
He did not make himself a poet,
Did not expire, did not go mad.
But rather, by the spring air quickened,
He left the close rooms where he'd sickened
And, marmot-like, slept winter through.

Left hearth and double-windows too,
One clear, bright morning, to go pelting
Sledge-borne among the Neva's shore.
On the blue, broken, icy floor
The sunshine plays; the snow is melting,
Uptorn and grimy, on the streets.
But whither now across it fleets

40

Onegin? – You have guessed, replying
Beforehand; as you apprehend,
To *her*, Tatyana, he is flying,
My strange, incorrigible friend.
He walks in, like some corpse decaying,
Encounters no-one on his way in,
Enters the next room – no-one there –
Opens a door . . . What meets his glare?
What stops him in his tracks, heart bleeding?
The princess – sitting in full sight,
Still in her *négligée*, all white,
With cheek on hand, alone and reading
Some kind of letter, it appears,
Her gentle face awash with tears.

41

Ah, but in that swift flash, who could not
Have fathomed all her dumb distress?
Who our poor, younger Tanya would not
Have recognised in that princess?
Yevgeny, full of ruth, in madness
Fell at her feet, o'erwrought with sadness;
She said no word, and shuddered, yet
Her gaze upon Onegin set
With no surprise, no indignation.
His ailing, his extinguished look,
Beseeching air, and dumb rebuke
She marked; like some reincarnation
Of that once simple maid she seems,
With her young heart, her early dreams.

42

She stares at him, her eyes not moving
From his; nor does she bid him stand;
Nor from his thirsty lips, reproving,
Withdraws her unresponsive hand.
What visions through her mind are thronging?
The silent pause no more prolonging,
At last she speaks, in tranquil tone:–
'Enough; now, rise; with you, I own,
There must be open explanation.
Onegin – I'll recall for you
When in the garden avenue
We met, by fate. Your exhortation
I heard, submissive then and dumb;
But now, today, my turn has come.

43

'I then, Onegin, they may tell me,
Was better: – younger, too, was I!
I loved you then; but what befell me?
And your heart gave me – what reply?
What found I in it? Rigour, purely!
A loving, humble girl was surely
No novelty to you? confess:
And now my blood just freezes, – yes,
Simply your icy look recalling,
And, heavens! that sermon that you gave . . .
Blameless, you managed to behave
With honour, in that hour appalling.
You acted right by me, I vow.
With all my soul, I thank you now.

44

'Is it not true that then, out yonder,
Far from the busy world's repute,
You liked me less as I grew fonder?
Then, why come now to persecute?
Why mark me down? Is this the reason,–
That I now figure, in due season,
In such high circles? That today

I'm rich and famous, as they say,
And have a husband maimed in fighting,
So that we are caressed at Court?
That all would notice and report
Any disgrace of my inciting?
That my disgrace is what you seek –
And irresistible mystique?

45

'I weep now. But, if an abiding
Thought of your Tanya haunts you still
Know this:– your stinging words, your chiding
And your discourse, so stern, so chill,
Were better, could the choice be offered,
Than this insulting passion proffered,
Than all these letters, all these tears.
Then, you showed reverence for my years;
At least you had some pity for me,
For my young, girlish reverie:
But now! – what brings you here? I see
You kneeling at my feet, before me.
How can you, with your mind and heart,
Stoop to play this ignoble part?

46

'This pomp, which all in tinsel dresses
The life that I abhor so much;
My evenings, stylish house, successes
In the world's eddy – what are such
To me, Onegin? I'd surrender
Gladly, this minute, all the splendour,
Glitter and vapour, noise, parade
Of frippery in masquerade,
For our poor house . . . the garden by it
Left wild . . . that bookshelf; for the place
Where first I saw Onegin's face;
Ay, for that burial-ground so quiet,
Where my poor nurse reposes now
Beneath her cross and shadowing bough.

47

'Oh, happiness – we might have known it! . . .
We nearly did . . . Now destiny
Has sealed my fate; though – I must own it –
I may have acted foolishly.
My mother wept, adjured, besought me.
Poor Tanya! whatso fortune brought me,
To me was all the same; and so
I married. Now, I beg you, go;
Please leave me. Do as you are bidden.
I know your heart will be your guide
With all its honour and its pride.
I love you – can the truth be hidden? –
But now that I'm another's wife,
I shall stay faithful all my life.'

48

She left the room. Yevgeny, reeling,
Stands thunderstruck before the burst
Of tumult and tempestuous feeling
In which his heart is now immersed.
But what is this? – Spurs jingling gently,
Tatyana's husband makes his entry . . .
Acute embarrassment is nigh.
But here, my reader, you and I
Shall leave him, and our separation
Will last . . . for ever. Far have we
Proceeded in close company,
But that's enough. Congratulations –
We're home at last! Let's shout 'Hooray!' –
Not before time, I hear you say.

49

Dear reader, be you friend or foeman,
My feeling now is that we ought
To part in friendship and good omen.
Goodbye. Whate'er you may have sought
In reading through these trivial stanzas –
Memory's wild extravaganzas,
A change from work, impressive strokes,

Or silly little witty jokes,
Or, it may be, mistakes of grammar –
God grant within this book you find,
For fun, love or a dreamy mind
Or for the journalistic hammer,
Some crumb at least. Now you and I
Must go our separate ways. Goodbye.

50

And you, companion (of the oddest!),
Goodbye to you, my vision pure,
My vibrant, constant work – if modest.
Because of you I've held secure
All things that could delight a poet.
Flight from the stormy world? I know it.
Good conversation? That is mine.
Time speeds. It is a long, long time
Since Tanya, youthful and reflective,
And my Onegin next to her,
Came to me in a dreamy blur.
As to my novel's free perspective –
Hard though I scanned my crystal ball,
I could not make it out at all.

51

And what of those good friends who listened
To my first stanzas freshly made?
Some are no more and some are distant,
As Sadi said. Without their aid
Onegin's portrait has been painted.
What of the girl who first acquainted
Me with Tatyana, perfect, pure? . . .
Fate's been a-thieving, to be sure . . .
Blest he who leaves a little early

Life's banquet without eating up
Or seeing the bottom of his cup,
Who drops his novel prematurely,
Bidding it suddenly adieu,
As I Yevgeny Onegin do.

Based on a translation by
Oliver Elton

58 The Captive in the Caucasus

PART ONE

Throughout the village, by their doors,
Sit the Circassians at their leisure,
Caucasian sons, talking with pleasure
Of dire alarms and deadly wars,
The passing beauty of their steeds,
And all their thrilling, wild existence.
Of past days they recall the deeds,
The raids destroying all resistance,
Tricks of the cunning one who leads,
The sure and certain shaft that flies,   10
The sabres and the savage clashes,
The villages reduced to ashes,
And tender captives with dark eyes.

Their words flow through the still night air;
A misty moon goes floating past.
Then suddenly up to them there
Rode a Circassian, dragging fast
A youthful prisoner, roped and tied.
'A Russian!' the marauder cried.
The village, when his shout was heard,   20
Came crowding up, hard-spirited,
But not a word the prisoner said;
Cold, with a mutilated head,
Corpse-like, he stood and never stirred.

The hostile glares he cannot see,
He cannot hear the threats, the taunting.
A sleep hangs o'er him fatally.
With deadly cold his breath is haunted.

The captive youth, as time dragged on,
In heaviest oblivion lay   30
Till noonday sun above him shone
And burned him, brightening the day.
Life's spirit now thrust sleep away,
His lips gave forth a muffled moan
And at the sun's warmth-giving ray
He eased up, wretchedly alone.
Now he looks round with feeble eyes . . .
Impregnable, the mountains rise.
He sees them over him immense;
There tribes of robbers have their den   40
And Cherkess freedom sets its fence.
The youth recalled his bondage then,
A ghastly dream of fearful pains.
He listens – there, the sudden ring
From feet that they have bound in chains . . .
The ghastly sound said everything.
Before him nature's darkness fell.
O blessed liberty, farewell!
A slave.
              Behind their huts he lies,
Unguarded, a thorn-hedge beside him.   50
Every last tribesman is out riding.
The silent village slowly dies.
Before him lies a spreading waste
Of flat land, like a shroud of green.
A ridge of hills can just be seen,
With peaks monotonously spaced,
A road between them, all forlorn,
Is lost in the forbidding distance;   .
And the young captive's breast was torn
By thoughts of harrowing insistence . . .   60

That long road leads to Russia, where
He started out, an ardent boy,

So proudly and without a care –
The land where he first met with joy,
Where dearly in him love had thrilled,
Where he had suffered terribly,
Where through his wild life he had killed
All longing, joy, expectancy,
And better days, through memory,
Were in his jaded heart instilled.   70

The world and people he had weighed,
The worth of fickle life he knew,
For he had found friends' hearts untrue
And dreams of love from folly made.
Quite sickened, victimised for ever
By vain ways he had long despised,
By enmity two-tongued and clever
As well as slanders undisguised,
As Nature's friend, this world denying,
He left behind his native bounds   80
And sped away to distant grounds
With freedom's joyful spirit flying.

O freedom! In the desert void
You, even you alone he sought,
His feelings passion had destroyed,
Dreams and the muse he set at nought,
But moving ballads would engross
Him, written by your inspiration;
With faith and fervent supplication
He held your lofty idol close.   90

This is the end! Hope has, it seems,
No purpose on this earth revealed
And even you, last of his dreams,
You too from him now lie concealed.
A slave. Head on a stone nearby,
He waits, that with the evening gloom
The flame of his sad life might die;
He craves the shelter of the tomb.

Beyond the hills the sunlight steals.
Far off there comes a rumoured sound;   100
The village-folk are homeward bound,
Their scythes a-glitter, from the fields.
They're back; the houses come to light,
Then soon the racket and the riot
Die down, all in the shades of night
Embraced by an ecstatic quiet.
The mountain spring glints, far away,
And plunges from the stony steep.
Shroud-like, the stormy clouds array
Caucasian summits in their sleep . . .   110
The moon above is shining clear
But, in the deep peace, who comes here?
What feet so stealthily have strayed?
The Russian started, his eyes meeting
A tender but unspoken greeting;
Here stands a young Circassian maid,
Whom he, without a word, inspects.
This is a false dream, he reflects,
A mean trick which fatigue has played.
Dimly the moonlight on her dwelt   120
As she, with pitying devotion
Set in her soothing smile, there knelt.
Towards his lips a milky potion
She, with her gentle touch, upraises.
But he spurns this healthgiving cup,
The magic of her lovely phrases
His thirsting spirit snatches up
And seizes on the maiden's gazes.
The strange words are beyond his ken,
And yet her longing gaze, warm cheek,   130
And yet her tender voice, these speak:
'Live!' and the prisoner lives again,
What strength remained he gathered, first.
Then, meek before the kind command,
Sat up and took the good bowl and
Soon slaked his overwhelming thirst.
And then once more upon the stone
A heavy burdened head he laid,

And yet the young Circassian maid
Still held his weak gaze, she alone.   140
A long, long time before him she
Sat pensively as if she would
With her unspoken sympathy
Console the prisoner all she could.
Her lips, perforce, time and again
Would open, start to speak to him;
And she would sigh and, now and then,
Tears in her eyes would overbrim.

    Day, shadowlike, succeeded day.
Chained near a flock out in the hills,   150
The prisoner passes them away.
There is a damp, dank cave that chills
And hides him from the summer blaze.
When, horned, the silver moon revives
And o'er the dark hill beams her rays
Down shady paths the girl arrives
And brings the prisoner wine, also
Sweet smelling honeycombs from hives,
Milk drinks and millet white as snow,
Shares secret suppers with him here,   160
Rests gazes on him soft and tender,
Commingles with her speech unclear
The words which eyes and signs engender,
Sings him those songs the mountains lend her
Or Georgian songs, gay as can be,
And to an eager memory
She now commits the foreign tongue.
Within her maiden's heart had sprung
First love and the first taste of bliss;
But the sharp pleasures of the young   170
Had left the Russian long ere this.
He could not make his heart reply
To such a love, childlike and frank.
Perhaps from memories he shrank
Of love forgotten and gone by.

    Our youth will not be swift to wither
Nor will delights leave us apace,

And joys which we have not called hither
Still many times shall we embrace.
But you, our senses' living capture,   180
You, early stirrings of first love,
You, flame divine of burning rapture,
No more shall fly here from above.

    It seemed the hopeless prisoner's days
Became a dull accustomed drag.
The ache of bonds, the rebel's blaze
Deep down he hid. His steps would flag
'Twixt beetling rock and sullen crag
Out in the early morning chill.
His searching eyes would turn to view   190
Each massive-standing, distant hill,
Grey-topped or rosy-tinged or blue.
What scenes magnificently rise!
The snows' own everlasting altars
With peaks appearing to the eyes
A cloudy chain that never falters;
A giant shining in their ring,
Two-headed, icy-crowned on high,
There Elbrus, huge, gigantic thing,
Stood white upon the light-blue sky.   200
When thunder, heralding a storm,
Banged dull and boomed, upon the hill
How often sat the prisoner's form
High up above the village, still!
Dark, smoky clouds beneath him swirled
And dust from off the steppe was whirled,
While in among the rocks the deer
Sought shelter, scampering in fear;
The eagles soared from crags, each brother
Across the heights called to another,   210
And all the sounds from cows to horses
The tempest's voice arose to smother . . .
Then rain and hail down valley courses
Were flung with lightning from the pother!
In waves which scoured the steeps in flight,

The stones of centuries displacing,
The rainy torrents would come racing –
But the prisoner from his mountain height,
Beyond the thundercloud, alone,
Would wait there for the sun's return,   220
And past the tempest's reach, unblown,
He'd listen to its feeble moan
With a certain joyful unconcern.

    The mind, though, of the European
These wondrous folk could not help heeding.
The hillsmen's faith, their ways, their breeding
The captive looked most curiously on
And loved their life's simplicity,
War-thirst and friendly fellowship,
Their body movements fast and free,   230
Fleetness of foot and strength of grip;
For hours he'd watch, and never stop,
One of these lithe Circassian folk,
O'er ranging steppe and mountain-top,
In shaggy cap and raven cloak,
Bend to the pommel, stirrup-cup
Upholding him in shapely stance,
Fly, effortlessly leaping up,
To learn war's methods in advance.
The splendour of them he admired,   240
For war or everyday attired.
To go well-armed they are inclined,
Out of both pride and peace of mind,
With mail, Kuban bow, quiver too,
With dagger, arquebus, lasso
And that true love of theirs – the sabre –
In times of leisure and of labour.

    No weight can cumber a Cherkess,
He holds it all, on foot or horse
Ever the same, and nothing less,   250
A staunch, unconquerable force,
This man the carefree Cossacks dread,
His wealth is in a lively steed

Which mountain herds have nursed and bred,
True, patient and a friend indeed.
In thick grass or in cavern biding
With him the cunning robber lies,
Then, like a sudden shaft outriding,
He sees a traveller and he flies,
The fight in one sure flash deciding   260
With a single mighty stroke; the rover
Towards abysmal mountain spaces
Soon in the soaring noose jerks over.
Full speed the flying charger races,
With fiery courage overflowing,
Through marsh and pinewood, through all places,
O'er bushes, crags and chasms going.
Behind him runs a trail of blood,
A thudding through the desert sweeps,
He meets a grey-topped, roaring flood   270
And dives into the seething deeps;
The rover, flung down, in his fall
Gasps in the waters, mud and all,
Craves death, for he can stand no more,
And death appears before his eyes . . .
But, arrow-like, the great steed flies
And bears him to the foaming shore.

Or, seizing some horned stump, flung down
Amidst a storm into the race,
When moonless night's dark shadows place   280
Upon the hills their burial gown,
Then, draping them on old roots or
Across the boughs, he will bestrow
All his accoutrements of war,
His helmet, armour, quiver, bow,
His cloak and shield, – and after it
Will plunge into the speeding flow,
A man of silence and of grit.
The night is black. This roaring course
Bears him upon her mighty force;   290
Secluded river banks pass by
Where up on burial mounds raised high

Stand Cossacks, leaning on their spears.
Each on the quick, black river peers;
And past them, darkly in the mist,
There swims a well-armed terrorist.
Cossack, what do you think about?
Old fights recalled from bygone days,
The fatal field, the camp set out,
The regiments in prayer and praise,   300
Your homeland? O, insidious dreaming!
Free villages your fathers knew,
Your hearth, the Don serenely streaming,
The war, the lovely girls – adieu!
The secret foe lands, moors his craft
And from his quiver comes an arrow.
The Cossack by the swishing shaft
Is toppled from the bloodstained barrow.

Yet when the peaceful kin together
Into their fathers' dwelling go   310
And our Cherkess, in stormy weather,
Sits by the embers burning low
And, in the hilly wastes out late,
A stranger comes here, tired indeed,
And, jumping from his trusted steed,
Sits timidly beside the grate,
Then the good-hearted host stands up
And with a friendly welcome sign
Offers his guest a fragrant cup
Of good *chikhir*, their own red wine.   320
The hut smokes; under a damp cloak
The passing stranger's sleep is sweet.
He leaves next morning the retreat
Of these most hospitable folk.

And always at bright Bairam-tide
There gathered crowds of their young men
And they would sport and sport again.
First, taking quivers well supplied,
And using shafts with feathered wings
The eagles in the clouds they shot;   330

Impatient ranks of reckless things,
They would upon a sign descend
And, flashing deer-like o'er the ground –
Dust flooding all the plain around –
Charge thunderously, friend by friend.

    And yet a world which stays the same
Must weary hearts for warfare born,
And often freedom's idle game
By sports of cruelty was torn.
Thus swords gleamed grimly now and then   340
At feasts, with spirits madly high;
Slaves' heads into the dust would fly
To cheers from rapturous young men.

    The Russian, though, watched unconcerned
These merry sports, however gory,
Once he had loved the games, the glory,
And with a thirst for havoc burned.
Bound to a code of honour cruel
Oft had he seen the end ahead,
Unflinching, cool, in many a duel   350
Encountering the deadly lead.
Perhaps, in deep thoughts occupied,
He now recalled the time when he,
With trusty friends on every side,
Had revelled with them noisily . . .
If he regretted days long past,
The days deceiving hope at last,
And if his interested gaze
Their simple, harsh amusements sought
Or read what this true mirror taught   360
Of savage people and their ways,
He kept in deepest silence hidden
What stirrings in his heart might churn,
His lofty forehead was forbidden
The very slightest change or turn,
His courage and his unconcern
Amazed the dread Circassians' eyes;
His life of tender years they spared

And in soft whispered voices shared
Proud satisfaction with their prize.   370

PART TWO
Young mountain maid, you came to know
Life's sweet gifts to the happy-hearted;
Your eyes, all innocent, aglow,
The joyousness of love imparted.
When in the darkest night your friend
Kissed you with his unspeaking kiss,
Afire with longing and with bliss,
This earthly sphere you would transcend
And you would say, 'O captive dear,
Fill your despondent eyes with cheer,   380
Your head upon my bosom set,
Your homeland, liberty – forget.
I'll gladly hide myself with you,
King of my soul, out in the waste!
O love me; no-one hitherto
Upon my eyes his lips has placed;
To my unvisited bedside
Not one Circassian youth, black-eyed,
Has stolen when the night was still;
I am a girl identified   390
As lovely but of cruel will.
I know my future lot is picked;
My father and my brother strict
Would sell me, an unloving wife,
For gold into some village other,
I'll beg my father and my brother –
Or else find poison or the knife.
What magic power is this that should
Draw me to you, completely captured?
I love you, prisoner so good,   400
You hold my very soul enraptured.'

    He gazed with unexpressed regret
At her, so passionately stirred,
And, with the gravest thoughts beset,
Listened to every loving word.

His wandering thoughts allowed a throng
Of long-forgotten days to arise,
And bitter tears welled in his eyes
To gush down in a hail headlong.
Lead-like upon his heart was laid   410
That pain which hopeless love must bring.
Then finally before the maid
He poured forth all his suffering.

   'Forget me. I deserve, in truth,
No love of yours or ecstasy.
Waste not your priceless days with me,
Call to yourself another youth.
His love will then replace for you
My sad soul's cold inhabitance;
And he will value, good and true,   420
Your beauty and your lovely glance,
The ardour of your young girl's kiss,
Your fiery speeches fondly made.
I lack the longing and the bliss;
A prey to passions, here I fade.
You see the signs that sad love forms,
Dread signs of spiritual storms;
So leave my sight, but pity me
My miserable destiny!

   Why did you not, my hapless friend,   430
Come earlier before my sight
In days when my belief might blend
With hope and daydreams of delight?
It is too late: joyless am I,
The phantom shade of hope has flown;
Your friend has set his senses by.
To tenderness he is as stone.

   With such dead lips as mine, how grim
It is to answer living kisses,
To meet these eyes that over brim   440
With a sad smile as cold as this is!
When, wearied with a useless zeal,

My spirit sleeps beyond all bother
And one girl's hot embrace I feel,
How grimly I recall another! . . .

When you with movements soft and slow
My kisses eagerly devour
And love makes every passing hour
So swiftly and serenely go,
In stillness here I swallow tears   450
Distractedly, despondently,
I watch as, dreamlike, there appears
An image ever dear to me.
I call to it, towards it yearn.
No sight, no sound, no speech can win it.
Forgetting this, to you I turn,
Embracing still a secret spirit.
For which I weep tears in the waste;
It wanders with me everywhere
And covers me with dark despair   460
Upon my lonely spirit placed.

Go, then, and to my shackles leave me,
To solitary imaginings,
To tears and memories that grieve me,
For you can never share these things.
You've heard all that my heart can tell;
Forgive me . . . give your hand . . . farewell.
When women separate from men
They do not go on pining for them.
Love passes – passes into boredom.   470
Fair maidens fall in love again.'

Mouth-open, sobbing without tears,
There sat this girl of tender years,
Her steady misted eyes the token
Of a reproachfulness unspoken.
She trembled, pallid as a shade,
And in her lover's hands she laid
Her own hand chilling to the touch.

At last the pain of love was such
That she began to ask him sadly: 480

   'Oh Russian, Russian, tell me why,
Not knowing your heart, why did I
Commit myself to you so madly?
Not long have I lain on your breast
In ecstasy, and I have not
Spent many nights with pleasure blessed.
So miserable is my lot.
Oh, will they ever be repeated?
Has happiness departed hence? . . .
You, prisoner, might well have cheated   490
My youth and inexperience
(Albeit with some pity filled)
By silence and a false caress;
Your destined days I should have thrilled
By humble care and tenderness
And sleeping moments watched away
To guard my anguished loved one's rest;
You would not . . . But who *is* she, say,
This girl of yours, the loveliest?
Do you love her? Does she love you? . . .   500
Your sufferings are very clear . . .
You must forgive my sobbing here
And spare my grief from laughter, too.'

   She stopped, for many a moan and tear
Racked the poor girl, cramping her breast.
Her lips moved, speaking wordless blame.
She hugged his knees, now passionless.
Her breath with difficulty came.
The captive with a gentle touch
Raised up the wretched girl and said;   510
'Don't cry. Fate haunts me just as much,
My heart in agony has bled.
No, shared love I could never claim,
I loved, I suffered all alone;
I'll perish like a smoking flame,
In wasted valleys lost, unknown;
Far from my longed-for shores I'll die,

My coffin of this steppe-land made;
And here my banished bones shall lie
With heavy, rusting chains o'erlaid . . .'   520

Darkly the stars of night declined,
The limpid distance soon outlined
The mountains snowy-white amassed.
Heads bowed, eyes lowered, now at last
They parted, silently resigned.

Since then the slave has gone downcast,
Lonely the village sees him stray.
As dawn upon the skyline burns,
For ever raising day on day,
And night, too, follows night away,   530
In vain for liberty he yearns.
If in the bush a chamois darts
Or antelopes through mists go streaking
The shackles clank as up he starts
There to await the Cossack sneaking
Who plunders villages at night
And rescues bondsmen from their plight.
He calls about . . . There are no sounds
Except the waves that plash, tormented.
The animal when man is scented   540
Into the desert darkness bounds.

The Russian prisoner hears one day
A warcry in the hills; 'Away!
To horse! To horse!' They run, they shout,
And copper bridles jingle out,
Black is the cloak, the mail bright-metalled,
The saddled horses seethe, unsettled,
The village strains to go out raiding.
Then, wild sons of war, they run
In courses from the hills cascading   550
To ride the banks of the Kuban
To strike as only brute force can.

The village is at rest. Sunlit,
The watchdogs by the hovels slumber

And naked infants, coloured umber,
Run freely with their sportive wit.
Greatgrandsires in a circle sit,
Wreathed in blue pipe-smoke. Songs are sung.
The girls they hear (without a word)
Sing the refrain they've often heard   560
And feel their old men's hearts grow young.

CIRCASSIAN SONG

1

The roaring river surges on;
Night's silence on the hill reposes:
The Cossack's weary day is done;
He leans on his steel spear, and dozes.
Sleep not, O Cossack; in the gloam
The Chechens near the river roam.

2

A Cossack comes canoeing down,
Nets on the river-bottom hauling.
O Cossack, in the stream you'll drown,   570
Like little foundered children falling
Who bathe on hot days in the foam.
The Chechens near the river roam.

3

There by the sacred waters, see
Rich villages are in full flower.
The songs and dancing go with glee.
Run, Russian songsters, with all power;
Hurry, fair maidens, to your home.
The Chechens near the river roam.

The girls sang. Sitting by the shore,   580
The Russian dreams of flight once more,
But leaden chains still bind him thickly;
The river runs so deep and quickly . . .
In twilight now the steppe-land sleeps.

The craggy peaks are darkened: soon
On white huts in the village creeps
The radiance of a pallid moon.
The deer above the waters doze,
The late call of the eagle stills,
A dull and distant echo goes 590
From thundering horse-herds through the hills.
But then he heard a noise nearby,
The girl's veil flashed before his eye,
And grievously and pallidly
Towards the prisoner came *she*.
Her lips are seeking some fine speech,
Her eyes are brimming pain withal,
In long black waves her tresses fall
And to her breast and shoulders reach.
In one hand was a saw that gleamed, 600
The other a steely dagger bore,
The girl was on her way, it seemed,
To secret battles, deeds of war.
Her gaze upon the captive stayed,
'Run quickly,' said the mountain maid,
'The Chechens will not ever find you.
Hurry, lose not the hours of night;
The dagger . . . no-one will catch sight
Of your tracks in the dark behind you.'

In trembling hands the saw she clasped. 610
Towards his feet the maid descended;
Beneath the saw the iron rasped,
Down rolled a teardrop unintended –
The shackles clanked and fell aside.
'Now you are free,' the maiden cried,
'Run!' But her frenzied eyes avowed
The love whose rush had swept her over.
She suffered; and the wind was loud;
It whistled, whirling through her cover.
The Russian cried out, 'My dear lover! 620
I'm yours for ever, till I die.
This dreadful place let us both fly.
Run with me now . . .' 'No, Russian, no!

Gone is the sweetness life can bring;
I have known joy, known everything.
And all has passed; no traces show.
You loved another! Can it be?
Give her your love; go, seek her out;
Why should this anguish stay with me?
And what are all my cares about?   630
Farewell! Love with its blessed gains
Beside you every hour shall stand.
Farewell! Forget me and my pains;
Once more, the last time . . . give your hand.'

   He reached for the Circassian maid,
To her with risen heart he flew,
The parting kiss was long delayed
And sealed the loving union true.
Dejectedly they held hands, turning
To go down to the bank. All sleeps;   640
The Russian in the sounding deeps
Swims straight away, the waters churning,
Reaches the rockface opposite,
And tries to find a hold on it . . .
Then as the heavy waters smite
There comes a distant moaning shout . . .
Upon the wild shore he climbs out,
Looks back . . . The shores are painted bright,
Foam-flooded, of refulgent white;
But the young girl is seen no more,   650
Not on the hillside or the shore . . .
The shores are sleeping; all is dead . . .
But for a light breeze in the ears.
As moonlit waters splash ahead
A rippling circle disappears.

   He understood. His eyes reverted
To let a last farewell embrace
The fence, the village now deserted,
The fields, his herd's old pasture place,
Crags where his chains had wearied him,   660
The stream where his noon rest would be

When in the hills the Cherkess grim
Struck up his song of liberty.

The skies thinned from their deepest black,
The dark dale was o'erlaid by day.
Dawn rose upon a distant track,
The liberated captive's way.
Before him, through a misty veil
The Russian bayonets gleamed hard.
From mound to mound echoed the hail   670
Of Cossack sentries standing guard.

(1820–21)

59   The Godyssey, or The Deviliad
(Gavriiliada)

The Russian word Gavriiliada *is formed from the two proper nouns*
Gavriil (Gabriel) *and* Iliada (The Iliad). *The last syllable of the first one*
overlaps the first syllable of the second to form a new proper noun
meaning The Gabriel-Iliad. *The English equivalents do not overlap*
exactly, but God *overlaps with* Odyssey *and the* Devil *with* Iliad, *hence*
the new title. To use it is to demote Gabriel, who comes off best in the
poem (except for Mary, of course), but the roles of God and The Devil are
almost as important as his. In all three cases proper respect is paid to
Homer.

I know a young Jewess, and verily
The saving of her spirit I hold dear.
Come, captivating angel, come to me,
Accept my peaceful benediction here.
To save an earthly beauty I aspire!
Well pleased when loving lips upon me smile,
To God and Jesus Christ I play my lyre,
Singing to them my lays in pious style.
The churchy strains of these, my lowly chords,

May one day captivate her; if I'm right   10
On this maid's heart the Holy Ghost may light,
Of every heart and mind the Lord of Lords.

  Ah, sweet sixteen, chaste meekness overall,
Dark brows, two maiden's hillocks underneath
Those vestments, such a supple rise and fall,
A leg for love, a jewelled row of teeth . . .
But, Jewess, you are smiling. Why is this?
Why did a blush colour your features too?
No, no. Your thoughts are leading you amiss.
I was describing Mary, dear, not you.   20

  Deep in the fields, far from Jerusalem
And from young blades and every kind of fun
(For ruination does the fiend keep them),
A beauty, hid as yet from everyone,
Spent all her days in peace and fancy free.
Her spouse, an honourable man was he,
A bad woodworker, old and grey of hair,
A village workman and the sole one there.
Being both day and night much occupied
With spirit-level, trusty saw and chopper,   30
He was not often wont to glance aside
Upon the charms with which he'd been supplied.
That secret bloom which fate had deemed it proper
To destine for another kind of honour
Was but a stem, no blossoms dared grow on her.
A lazy spouse, with his old watering can
He never laved his bloom at morningtide.
With his pure maid lived this paternal man –
Her appetite was all he satisfied.

  But from the righteous heights of heav'n His glance   40
One day the Almighty turned in friendly fashion
Upon the girlish breast and shapely stance
Of this, His slave; and, sensing a hot passion,
In His omniscience wondrously profound
This worthy vineyard He proposed to bless,

Bringing to its forlorn, forgotten ground
Secret rewards – such as His bounteousness.

   And now night's silence wraps the fields around.
There in her corner Mary's sleep is sound.
The Almighty spake, and came into her dreams.   50
Now her horizon splits to its extremes,
The boundless deeps of heaven overbrim
In glory and intolerable glim
And hosts of angels stir and seethe in it.
There fly innumerable seraphim,
Here, plucking at their harps, are cherubim,
And all unspeaking the Archangels sit.
Beneath their azure wings their heads are bowed.
Before them, panoplied in dazzling cloud,
Lo, the Eternal Being's throne doth rise.   60
And lo! he flashes bright before their eyes.
All prostrate fall . . . The harping music dies . . .
Mary looks down and scarce can get her breath,
Atremble like a leaf with God, who saith,
'Sweet daughter of the world, its loveliest
Young maid, who art the hope of Israel,
Afire with love, I call on thee to dwell
With me in glory – this is my behest.
Prepare thyself to meet an unknown doom.
To his obedient slave shall come the groom.'   70

   The Lord's throne was adorned with cloud anew,
In winged legions spirits all upflew,
Once more did heavenly harps their music start . . .
With fondly folded arms and lips apart,
Thus Mary stands and faces heaven now.
But what's this, stirring, tempting her somehow,
Seducing her attentive eyes . . . to whom?
Which of the young men in the courtly throng
Can't tear his blue eyes from her all along?
The splendid garb, the helmet with its plume,   80
The glowing wings, the tresses gold and long,
The tall stance and the languid look, shamefaced,
All this was much to speechless Mary's taste.
He's won her heart, He stands out from the crowd.

Archangel Gabriel be very proud!
The scene dissolves. – Despite the children's plea
Thus from the cloth do all those shadows flee
That in a magic lantern have been born.

   The lovely maid woke in the early morn
And on her couch she nestled languidly.   90
The wondrous dream and gorgeous Gabriel
Nothing could from her memory dispel.
Dearly she wanted to love heaven's master
Whose words had given her a pleasant thrill,
In reverence to Him no one surpassed her,
But Gabriel, thought she, was nicer still.
Sometimes a general's wife is, just as she,
Attracted to a strait-laced adjutant.
What can we do? It's fate; all men agree,
The academic and the ignorant.   100

   Let us now talk of love's strange character
(The only talk I understand). In days
When at the sight of someone's ardent gaze
We feel our blood immediately astir,
When false desire with its tormenting anguish
Embraces us and leaves the spirit flagging
While after us comes, dogging us and dragging,
The only thing for which we long and languish –
Is this not true? Among friends dear and young
We find a confidant, for him we reach,   110
Tormenting passion's mystifying tongue
We then interpret with ecstatic speech.
And when we've seized in flight above our head
The winged moment bringing heaven's rapture
And every moment we have sought to capture,
Bending a blushing beauty to the bed,
When we forget love's pain, how we were stricken,
And nothing's left to long for – then, at that,
The recollection of it all to quicken,
We love to find our confidant and chat.   120

   And Thou, Lord, Thou didst know that agitation,
And Thou didst burn like us, O God above.

The great creator cooled to His creation,
The prayers of heav'n seemed a dull occupation –
He sat composing many a psalm of love,
And loud He sang: 'I love thee, Mary mine,
My immortality drags dully by . . .
Where are my wings? To Mary I shall fly
And on my beauty's breast I shall recline . . .'
And all such speeches as He could compile –   130
He loved the multicoloured, Eastern style.
Calling His favourite, Gabriel, to His side,
He told, in prose, how He adored His beauty.
But what they said the Church sees fit to hide,
The Gospeller did not quite do his duty.
There's one Armenian legend, though; in it
The King of Heav'n, while praising all anent him,
Told Gabriel for Mercury He meant him,
Cognizant of his talent and his wit.
So down to Mary that same night He sent him.   140
Some other honour the Archangel sought.
He had enjoyed full many a happy mission
And notes and news he'd taken out and brought.
'Twas profitable – yet he had ambition.
This son of glory hid his disposition
And forced himself to serve, helpful and sure,
The King of Heav'n . . . down here we say 'procure'.

    But Satan, the old enemy, sleeps not!
Out in the wide world he heard, as he strayed,
That God's eye was upon a Jewish maid,   150
A lovely girl, and it would be her lot
To save our kind from Hell's torment eternal.
Greatly did this annoy the fiend infernal
And he took certain steps . . . The Almighty, though,
Sat up in heaven, filled with sweet dismay,
Forgetting the unmarshalled world below.
Without Him everything went its own way.

    But what is Mary doing? Where is she,
The spouse of Joseph so deprived of pleasure?

There in her garden sadly, pensively,   160
She spends the hour of her so spotless leisure
And waits once more for sleep's sweet tyranny.
A well-loved image weighs upon her soul
Which sadly soars to Gabriel, its goal.
Beneath cool palms, beside a purling stream
My lovely heroine begins to dream.
The fragrant blooms give her no joy, not they,
The gurgling, limpid waters are not gay . . .
But then she sees a serpent, all agleam,
In gorgeously alluring scales arrayed,   170
Swaying above her in the branchy shade.
Says he, 'O child of heav'n, beloved lass!
Stay! I'm your captive, slave to your control.'
Wonder of wonders! What has come to pass?
Who was it spoke to Mary, simple soul?
Who was it but the fiend himself, alas?

    The lovely snake, the varied spread of flowers,
The call, the fiery devil's eyes, all these
Took Mary's fancy now. As if to please
With joy a young heart in its idle hours   180
She set on Satan her soft glance and thus
Began to talk, though it was dangerous:
'Snake, who are you? These sung charms, I perceive,
This brilliance and this beauty and this gaze,
These mean that you are he, I do believe,
Who to the mystic tree lured sister Eve
And bent her, wretched girl, to sinful ways.
You ruined her, so young and so naive,
All Adam's kin and us with such behaviour.   190
We were forced down into an evil pit.
Aren't you ashamed?'
                        'The priests fool you, that's it.
I did not ruin Eve. I was her saviour!'
'Saviour! From whom?'
                        'From God.'
                                     'A vicious foe!'
'He was in love.'
                        'Now listen here, take care!'

'He burned with passion for her . . .'
                              'Hush!'
                                        'It's so,
She was in dreadful danger.'
                          'I say no,
You're lying, snake!'
                  'My God!'
                            'Please do not swear!'
'But hear me out!'
                  Now Mary thought, 'Indeed
It may be bad, alone here in the garden,   200
Slyly the slanders of a snake to heed.
For trusting Satan's words can there be pardon?
Th Omnipotent, though, guards and loves me too,
The Lord is good and surely won't undo
His slave – for what? For chatting – surely not!
Besides He will preserve me from mistake
And it's a pretty modest-looking snake.
Can this be sin or evil? Tommy rot!'
She thought thus, lent an ear, and for a spell
Forgot about her love and Gabriel.   210
The devil superciliously unwreathed
His rattling tail, and arched his neck and thither
He dropped before her from the branch, aslither.
Flames of desire into her breast he breathed.
Said he,
          'That story (Moses' point of view)
To square with mine I shall not even try.
He used a fiction to enslave the Jew.
They listened to him and his whopping lie.
God recompensed his words, his humble mind;
Moses became a man of note indeed.   220
But I'm no court historian you'll find,
For the high rank of prophet I've no need.

  All other lovely women, to be sure,
Should envy you your eyes, such fiery ones;
Yes, you were born, O Mary so demure,
To stagger and astonish Adam's sons,
To make their easy hearts bow down to you,

To turn your smile upon them bringing bliss,
To send them frantic with a word or two,
To fancy love or not to fancy – this   230
Shall be your lot. Young Eve like you was made
Demure, intelligent, so sweet a bloom,
But loveless in the garden and in gloom.
Always alone together, man and maid
Upon the banks of Eden's lucid streams
Lived peaceably, and innocent, it seems.
Monotonous and tedious were their days.
The shady grove, their youth, their idle ways,
All failed to bring them love of any sort;
They wandered hand in hand, they ate and drank,   240
They yawned the days away, their nights were blank.
No *joie de vivre*, no impassioned sport.
What can you say? That tyrant so unfair,
The Jewish God, of sullen, jealous air,
Himself in love with Adam's friend, alone
Was keeping her to be his very own.
What joy in this, what honour is arisen!
Stay there in heav'n, as if you were in prison,
Sit at His feet and pray, it is your duty,
Sing praises to Him, wonder at His beauty,   250
Look not on others with a stealthy eye
Nor whisper to an archangel nearby.
Poor girl! This fate must finally await her
As a companion of the Lord creator.
What follows? For your pains, for being bored,
Sacristans' wheezy songs are your reward,
Candles, old women's prayers that annoy,
The censer's smoke and, diamond inlaid,
An ikon by some painter of the trade.
An enviable fate! How full of joy!   260

    My pity for the charming Eve was such
That I resolved to spite the Lord. I meant
To stir the couple's sleep up very much.
You must have heard the tale of how it went.
Two apples dangling from a wondrous bough,
(Love's happy, warming symbol), these somehow

Brought a new daydream vaguely to her view
And woke her dimly to an inward yearning.
For the first time her loveliness she knew,
Her body's thrill, her heart's disturbing churning,   270
The nakedness of her young husband too.
I watched them! Love, the science I had made,
I watched it as it wonderfully started,
As deep into the woods my pair departed . . .
Where very soon their eyes, their hands had strayed . . .
Between his young wife's lovely legs aseeking,
Solicitous, inexpert and unspeaking,
Adam went off on an enraptured course,
Within him furiously a fire was lit,
He wondered at the pleasurable source,   280
His spirit boiled and he was lost in it . . .
For Eve the wrath divine no longer mattered,
She felt herself on fire, her hair was scattered,
Her lips were just aquiver as she clung
To Adam and responded with a kiss.
In tears of love and senseless, after this
She lay 'neath shady palms; the young earth flung
Her blossoms o'er the lovers, man and miss.

O day of bliss! The husband newly crowned
Caressed his wife from dawn to dusk, he did,   290
And in the darkness scarcely closed a lid.
Their leisure time was well adorned, they found!
But God broke up their joy and, as you know,
From paradise for ever made them go,
Expelling them both from this lovely clime
Where they had lived so long without offence,
Where they had spent their days in innocence,
Embraced by lazy stillness all the time.
But I had shown them sensuality,
The joyful rights of youth that they were missing,   300
Bodily languor, passion's tears and glee
And words breathed out with tenderness, and kissing.
Now kindly tell me, whom have I betrayed?
Because of me has Adam cause to grieve?
I think not! And I know one thing of Eve:

I was her friend before; such have I stayed.'

At this the devil stopped. Without a word
All Satan's wily tales Mary had heard.
'Perhaps it's true,' she thought, 'the devil's story.
I've heard that not with honours or with glory   310
Can bliss be got; it can't be bought with gold.
It's love that must be found, I've heard it told . . .
It's love! But what is love and how and why?'
And in the meantime her young ear and eye
Missed nothing in the picture Satan drew,
What deeds were done, their causes, passing strange,
The bold style and the images' free range
(We all delight in finding something new).
From vague beginnings – as the time went on –
Her risky thoughts gained greater definition   320
And suddenly the snake seemed to have gone.
Before her was another apparition.
Mary now sees a young man fair and sleek
Before her very feet. He does not speak
But glints his eyes superbly; in addition,
He asks for something eloquently and
He offers a small flower with one hand.
The other in her plain dress is afumble
And quickly up inside her vestment steals
And playfully a gentle finger feels   330
In there for secret pleasures. Mary reels.
It's wondrous, new and something of a jumble.
But in the interim a shameless flush
Upon her virgin cheeks begins to play,
Hot languor and an anxious panting rush
Now cause young Mary's breast to heave away.
Silent is she. Soon she was drained of strength.
Breathless, she closed her weary eyes at length,
Inclined her head upon the devil's breast,
Sighed, 'Ah!' and on the grass sank down to rest.   340

My dear friend! You to whom I once consigned
My early dreams of hope and my first yearning,
The lovely girl to whom I once was kind,

Will you forgive my memories returning,
The pleasures of my younger days, my sin,
Those evenings when your family was in,
When, near your strict, infuriating mother
With secretive unrest I caused you bother,
Enlightening your spotless beauty by it?
I took your ready hand and set it right 350
To cheat sad separation and excite
A sweet relief during those hours of quiet,
A maiden's agonising, sleepless night.
But now your days of youth are at an end,
Your smile has flown away, your lips have paled,
In its full bloom your loveliness has failed . . .
Will you forgive me now, my dearest friend?

You, Mary's evil foe, the sire of sin,
For everything she did yours was the fault,
You loved it when she fell to your assault, 360
Your wicked sport, this was the origin,
This roused the spouse of the Omnipotent,
Your boldness shook her, she was innocent.
What glory you may proudly revel in!
Catch all you can . . . the hour is just ahead!
Now day is darkening, twilight's ray is dead.
Peace. Then down o'er the weary maiden springs
The soaring archangel with swishing wings,
Love's emissary, heaven's brilliant child.

'Twas Gabriel. From horror at the sight 370
The lovely maiden hid her face in fright . . .
The Prince of Darkness rose before him, riled.
'Proud creature,' says he, 'You in bliss do dwell.
Who sent for you? Why come you from up there,
The courts of heav'n, the ethereal upper air?
Why do you break the secret, silent spell
And spoil the business of a loving pair?'
But with a frown the jealous Gabriel
Thought this was rude and a bad joke as well. 380
Quoth he, 'Mad devil, as the heavens fair,
You hopeless exile, wild and wicked one,

Sweet Mary's charms you've tempted and undone.
You question me? What liberties you take!
Slave, shameless rebel, let me see you run
Or I shall turn on you and you shall quake!'
'I quake at no one coming from your court,
At God's subordinates, that humble sort
Who but procure for the Omnipotent!'
The devil spake thus, blazed malevolent,   390
Puckered his brow, with narrowed eyes beneath.
Biting his lips, he smashed him in the teeth.
A cry rang out and Gabriel went reeling
And there he was upon his left leg kneeling.
But soon a new-found ardour helped him rise
And he hit Satan, much to his surprise,
Right on his temple. Satan cried out, paling.
They fell into each other's clutches, and
The devil, Gabriel, neither prevailing,
Wheeled, interlocked, across the meadowland,   400
Their chins into each other's chests they drove,
Their legs and arms conjoined and crisscross running.
With brute force or with scientific cunning
To drag the other after how they strove!

You will recall that field, I'm sure you will,
Where once, my friend, on many a spring day,
We cut our classes and we played our fill,
We fought formidably. What splendid play!
Weary, forgoing comments good or bad,
The angels fought together in this way.   410
King of the Underworld, he, husky cad,
Groaned vainly his sharp foe to overwhelm
And finally, to end it at one go,
He knocked off the archangel's plumed helm,
The golden helm with diamonds aglow.
He grasps the enemy by his soft hair
And from behind him with a mighty arm
Bends him to the dry ground. In all his charm
Mary sees the Archangel fastened there
And can but tremble, speechless, for his sake.   420
Hell cheers delightedly the devil's break

But Gabriel's quick thinking saved his skin,
He gave the devil's vital part a bite
(A useless part in almost any fight),
That puffed up member he had used to sin.
The devil cried for mercy, giving in,
And limped off back into the dark of Hell.

　The wondrous fight, the terrible pell-mell,
The maid had watched all breathless with distress.
Now when towards her, fresh from his success,　　　　　　　　430
The Archangel benevolently turned,
With flooding fires of love his features burned,
His spirit overbrimmed with tenderness.
Ah, what a pretty picture – the Jewess!

　The emissary blushed and then gave voice
In words divine to his strange feelings, thus:
'O Mary, full of innocence, rejoice,
Love be with you, lady most beauteous,
A hundred times your holy child is blest,
He'll save the world and cast down Hell, he will . . .　　　440
But by my candid soul be it confessed
His sire's a hundred times more blessed still.'
He bent his knee before her and he pressed
Her hand with gentle tenderness at this . . .
The lovely maiden looked down with a sigh
And Gabriel embraced her with a kiss.
Confused, she reddened, but without reply.
He dared to lay his hand upon her breast.
'Oh, leave me, please!' came Mary's whispered cry.
But in that instant his embrace suppressed　　　　　　　　450
Her last pure urge to moan or to protest.

　What now? The jealous Lord, what will he say?
My lovely ones, you really needn't mind.
You who confer in love, O womankind,
With happy artistry you know the way
To fox a bridegroom and to take him in,
Even the probing looks of those who know,
To cover up the signs of pleasant sin

With garb of innocence for outward show.
Each mother well instructs her naughty daughter   460
In shamed embarrassment, pretended pains.
A falsified timidity she feigns
On that key night, playing out what was taught her.
By dawn she rallies, somewhat more vivacious,
She rises pale, and limps, weak from the strain.
The spouse exults, but mother whispers, 'Gracious!'
An old friend has come tapping on the pane.

Now Gabriel with his most pleasant tiding
Wings his way homeward through the heavens gliding.
Magnanimous, though anxious, God began   470
To greet the one in whom He'd been confiding:
'What's new?' 'Well, I've done everything I can.
I've told her.' 'Yes, what did she say?' 'She will.'
At this the Lord of Heaven's tongue was still.
Leaving His throne He twitched His brows and thence
Dismissed them all like Homer's God of yore
Who kept his many sons in deference.
But that Greek faith has gone for evermore.
There is no Zeus today. We have more sense!

She thrilled at the fresh memory returning.   480
In Mary's nook the stillness was complete
As she reclined upon her rumpled sheet,
Her soul ablaze with rapture and with yearning.
Her young breast feels a new and searing flare.
Softly she calls to Gabriel above her.
The secret gift of love she must prepare
And so she kicks off her nocturnal cover,
Looks down and smiles, as does a happy lover.
Her own sweet nakedness affords her bliss,
She marvels that she is so fair as this.   490
Into a gentle reverie she sinks,
Lovely and languid, then she sins soon after.
Serenely from the cup of joy she drinks.
Ah, wicked Satan, I can hear your laughter!
But what is this? Here comes a feathered dove,
White-winged, in through her window from above,

And all aflutter round and round he goes,
Crooning as best he can sweet melodies.
Then, flying down between the maiden's knees,
He settles, quivering, above his rose,   500
He pecks it, crawls about, turns to and fro,
His tiny beak and feet all on the go.
It must be He! On Mary it soon dawned
That in this dove she had another guest.
She gave a cry, her knees together pressed,
She sighed and trembled, and she wept and fawned.
But no, the dove his victory pursues,
In ecstasies of love he quivers, coos,
Then falls away, by sleep gently embraced,
His shading wing upon love's flower placed.   510

   A weary Mary, as he flew away,
Thought, 'Ah, what fun and games I've had today!
That's – one, two, three. They're really not too bad!
I've weathered it, I think I can record.
Together in a single day I've had
The Devil, one Archangel and the Lord.'

   And afterwards the Lord, we can't deny it,
Claimed as His own the Jewish maiden's son.
But fate made Gabriel the lucky one;
He kept on seeing Mary on the quiet.   520
Like many others Joseph was content,
Towards his spouse he stayed all innocent
And he loved Jesus Christ as his own boy
For which the Lord rewarded him with joy.

   Amen, amen! My tale must end. But how?
My roguery of old I leave off now.
You, winged Gabriel, I serenade.
Their hymn to you my humble strings have played,
This so sincere, salvationary air.
Now keep me safe and listen to my prayer!   530
Till now I've been a heretic in love,
Young goddesses insanely worshipping,
The demon's friend, a faithless, mad young thing.

Give my repentance blessing from above!
I now assume intentions that are kinder.
I'll change. A certain Helen I have seen,
As sweet as gentle Mary was I find her
And of my soul she is for ever queen.
With charming accents all my words inspire,
Teach me the secret means by which to please   540
And in her bosom kindle love's desire –
Or else I'll turn to Satan on my knees!
But days fly past and time will bring the grey,
Upon my head will scatter silver gently.
With a nice wife my solemn wedding day
Will at the altar join me permanently.
O Joseph's comforter and handsome friend!
I pray you here upon my bended knee,
You who do guard all cuckolds and defend,
I pray you, when that time arrives, bless me   550
And give me blessed patience all my life.
I pray you may I ever and again
Sleep peacefully, enjoy a faithful wife,
Find peace at home and love my fellow men.

(1821)

60   The Bronze Horseman

INTRODUCTION
Gazing upon the watery waste,
He, with his mighty visions, faced
The farthest deeps. Broad and remote,
The river carried, as it raced,
One little, miserable boat.
The swampy banks were mossy green
With dark huts few and far between,
The homes of lowly Finnish folk.
The forests through their misty screen,
Where hidden sunbeams never broke,   10
Were murmuring.

And he reflected:
'To menace Sweden from this place
A city here shall be erected,
Thrown in our haughty neighbour's face.
A window into Europe we
Shall cut, by Nature's own decree,
And firmly hold our sea-shore station.
Borne here across the unknown main
All vessels we shall entertain
And freely spread our celebration.'   20

A century saw the city's birth:
A lovely wonder of the North,
From darkest woods and swampy earth
Magnificently rising forth.
Where Finnish fishermen before,
Step-sons of Nature, all alone,
Stood sadly on the shallow shore
And cast into the depths unknown
Their rotting nets – in this place now
Along the living banks see how   30
Huge, shapely buildings throng and rise,
Tower and palace; vessels race
In crowds from earth's remotest place
To quaysides rich with all supplies.
The Neva now was clad in stone,
New bridges crossed the water, while,
Dark decorating every isle,
Green were the gardens which had grown.
The capital, of younger life,
Outshone the Moscow that had been,   40
As an ascendant ruler's wife
Outshines the purpled, widowed queen.

O, Peter's work, I love you so!
I love your stateliness and strength,
The Neva's soft majestic flow,
The granite bordering her length,
Your iron railings' strong design,
And through the thoughtfulness of night

Your limpid twilight's moonless shine.
When in my room I stay to write   50
Or sit, without a lamp, to read,
The sleeping streets shine clear indeed,
Vast masses emptied of their people;
Bright, too, the Admiralty steeple.
The darkness is denied possession
Of this, the golden firmament;
Dawn follows dawn in swift succession;
Night's borrowed half-hour soon is spent.
I love your cruel winter, too,
The still air and the frosty shiver,   60
Girls' cheeks with more than rosy hue,
The sledging down the Neva river,
The brilliance, noise and talk there is
At balls; the single-fellow's turn
To feast, when glasses foam and fizz
And in the punch the blue flames burn.
I love, in lively, warlike duty,
Cadets upon the Martian field,
Footsoldiers, cavalry, who yield
Identical, unchanging beauty,   70
The rippling, orderly array
Of banners torn, victorious ones,
Their helmets, wrought with shining bronze,
Shot through by bullets in the fray.
I love you, capital of Mars,
When fortress cannons smoke and roar
To welcome to the House of Tsars
A son, the Northern Queen's gift; or
To greet new victories in war
And raise triumphant Russian voices;   80
Or when the Neva starts the motion
Of cracked blue ice towards the ocean
And, sensing Spring is near, rejoices.

O Peter's town, like Russia, here
Stand splendidly and firmly founded!
Peace with the elements is near,
The elements which you confounded.

The wrath and chains of yesteryear
May Finland's waters soon forget,
Nor with their futile rage upset   90
Tsar Peter's everlasting sleep.

   A time of dread there was. We keep
A memory of it not yet old . . .
And of these times, my reader-friend,
The story shall I now unfold
From sorry start to grievous end.

PART ONE
   On Petrograd the dark mists rose,
November blew and autumn froze.
The noisy Neva splashed ahead
And in her shapely confines heaved,   100
As does a sick man, in his bed
Tossing and turning, unrelieved.
And in the midnight darkness rain
Beat bitterly upon the pane.
The keening tempest howled and squalled.

   From visiting now homeward came
A youth. Yevgeny was his name.
Our present hero shall be called
By such a title, since its sound
Delights the ear; my pen has found   110
Before a friendly air about it.
His surname? We can do without it,
Though years ago it might have been
In something of a bright position,
And in the hands of Karamzin
A great sound in our land's tradition;
And yet the world and tongues of men
Do not recall it now as then.
Somewhere our hero is employed,
The great he chooses to avoid,   120
Lives in Kolomna, never weeping
For ages lost or kinsfolk sleeping.

Yevgeny, then, arriving home,
Took off his overcoat, undressed,
Lay down, but could not sleep or rest,
So widely did his wild thoughts roam.
What did he think about? That he
Was poor; that honest toil might see
Him grow to be of good repute
And of the self-sufficient kind;   130
That God might further contribute
To fill his pocket and his mind.
That many a lucky man displays
A lack of wit and lazy ways
And yet lives easy and secure!
That he had worked two years together.
He also thought about the weather,
Relentless still; by now, for sure,
From off the river, as it lifted,
The Neva bridges had been shifted: 140
He and Parasha some few days
Would follow separated ways.
Yevgeny gave a heartfelt sigh
And set off dreaming like a poet:

'Marriage? Why should I never know it?
Life would be hard, of course, but I,
With youth and health, am well prepared
To labour night and day, unspared;
And I shall find a way to build
A humble shelter, plain to see,   150
Where all Parasha's cares are stilled.
And in a year or two, maybe,
I'll get a little job and give
Parasha care of where we live
And also of the children; thus
We shall live, and, hand in hand,
Together till the grave we'll stand.
Our grandchildren shall bury us . . .'

Thus did he dream that night, alone
In sadness; if the wind and rain   160

Would only ease their plaintive moan
And not attack the window-pane
With such a fury . . .
                Heavy-eyed,
At last he slept. The stormy grey
Fades from the misty night outside
And thins before a pale new day . . .
A day of horror!
            All that night
The Neva faced both storm and sea,
Crushed by their wild stupidity,
Until she could no longer fight . . .   170

By morning crowds were teeming by
Along her banks to watch and wonder
At waters splashing mountains high
And foaming furiously asunder.
But gales were blowing from the bay
To block the Neva; coming round,
She stormed and seethed and in her way
The islands, one by one, were drowned.
The weather raged with greater force,
The Neva, rising in her course,   180
A roaring cauldron, swirled and spat,
Then, like a savage beast, leapt at
The city . . . All that stood before
Recoiled and ran. The space around
Soon stood deserted. Underground
The cellars filled before the spate.
Canals gushed up at every grate.
Petropolis was soon to be
Waist-deep, like Triton, in the sea . . .

A siege! The wicked waters strike,   190
Climbing through windows, burglar-like.
The sterns of boats in full career
Smash panes. Now hawkers' trays appear
With covers soaked; beams, roofs go past
From broken huts; cheap things amassed
By poor, pale beggars, few by few;

Storm-shattered bridges; coffins, too,
From steeping cemeteries exhumed,
Swim down the streets!
      The people fear
God's wrath and sense his judgement near. 200
Their food, their shelter, all is doomed!
Where shall they turn?
      In that dread year
The glorious Tsar, now at his rest,
Ruled Russia still. Then out came he,
Sad, stricken, on the balcony.
'The Tsars,' he said, 'may not contest
God's elements.' In deep remorse
He sat and watched, with pensive air,
Disaster take its evil course.
A lake had formed in every square, 210
With great, wide torrents rushing there
Down all the streets. The palace lay,
A sorry island now. The Tsar
Then spoke; and, hurrying away
To thoroughfares both near and far,
His generals went up and down,
In peril from the storming tide,
To save the people, terrified
And waiting in their homes to drown.

And at this time in Peter's square 220
A great, new corner-house stood, where,
Paw raised, each like a living cat,
Above the elevated entry
A pair of lions stood on sentry.
Astride one marble beast here sat,
Arms folded and without his hat,
Yevgeny, still and deathly white,
A wretched figure, filled with fright
– Not for his own sake. And although
A wave rose hungrily below, 230
Lapping the very shoes he wore,
Though winds began to howl and blow,
And lashed his face with rain, and tore

His hat away . . . he did not know.
His eyes were brimming with despair,
Fixed rigid on one place, to keep
A constant watch. Like mountains, there,
Arising from the angry deep,
The raging waters towered high,
The tempest howled there, sweeping by   240
With wreckage. Lord! There by the bay,
A stone's throw (alas! no more) away
From the water's edge, he seems to see
A plain fence and a willow-tree,
A little house in poor repair.
Parasha, whom he dreams of seeing,
Lives with her widowed mother there . . .
. . . Or has he dreamed them into being?
Is all life empty, merely worth
A dream where heaven mocks the earth?   250

And he, as if he were enchanted,
As if the marble held him planted,
Cannot climb down! At every quarter
Lies an unbroken stretch of water.
And with its back towards him, why!
Above the Neva's stormy course,
Rearing implacably on high,
One arm outflung across the sky,
The Idol straddles his bronze horse.

PART TWO
At length destruction was to pall   260
And then – the taste of fury cloying –
The Neva stole away, enjoying
Her very insolence and gall,
Indifferently letting fall
Her loot behind. In this way, too,
A robber and his vicious crew
Bursts on a village, sacking, routing,
Cutting, smashing; to screams and shouting,
Teeth-gritting clashes, frightened faces
And savage frenzy . . . Piled with loot   270

And fearing possible pursuit,
The weary vandal homeward chases
And strews his plunder down the street.

    The roadway, on the waves' retreat,
Lies open. My Yevgeny races,
His spirits sinking, bitter-sweet
With fear and hope, till he draws near
The torrent's half-subdued career.
But, filled with their victorious thrill,
The waters seethed with evil still,   280
As if a fire lay deep-concealed.
The Neva, foam flecked in her course,
Breathed heavily like some great horse
Galloping from the battlefield.
Yevgeny looks; a boat he spies
And runs up to this lucky prize,
Hailing the ferryman, and he,
Who ferries on without a care,
Agrees for only a modest fare
To row him through the fearsome sea.   290

    With stormy wave on stormy wave
Long did the expert oar contend;
Through them the crew, however brave,
Risked constantly a plunging grave
In such a craft, till . . . in the end
It reached the shore.
                  He rushes through
A well-known street to well-known places,
Not recognising what he faces,
Wretched before the awesome view!
With everything in disarray   300
And all torn down or swept away;
Some cottages stand all awry,
Some are in ruins, others lie
Demolished by the waves. All round
The scene is like a battleground,
With bodies strewn to left and right.
    Yevgeny, failing in his mind,

Weak from his agonising plight,
Runs straight to where he is to find
The hidden news, known but to fate, 310
As in a letter sealed up fast.
Down through the suburb quickly . . . wait,
Here is the bay, the house just past . . .
What's this? . . .
       He stopped dead in his track,
Retraced a step or two, came back.
He stares . . . moves on . . . another stare . . .
Shouldn't the house be standing there?
Here is the willow, but the gate . . .
Swept off . . . The house cannot be found!
With darkest cares to contemplate 320
He walks in circles, round and round,
Only to rend the air and rave.
Then, beating on his brow, he gave
A sudden laugh.
      Night's mist came down
And settled on the trembling town,
But late the people stayed awake,
Talking, wondering what to make
Of that past day.
      The rays of morn
From storm-clouds pallid now, and worn,
On a peaceful capital shone through. 330
The troubles of the day before
Had left no trace; a purple hue
Held the evil hidden and ignored.
The former order was restored.
Down streets where freedom had returned
Walked people coldly unconcerned.
Their shelter of the night forsaken,
Clerks left for work. Bold and unshaken,
The huckster opened up again
His cellar, pillaged by the flood, 340
Aiming to make his losses good
With profits made from other men.
And boats were lifted from the yard.

Already Count Khvostov, the bard
Beloved by Heaven, immortal master,
Was versifying the disaster
With which the Neva's banks were scarred.

My poor Yevgeny, wretched figure . . .
Alas! His mind was so hard pressed
It could not stand the awful rigour   350
Of all these shocks. The wild unrest
Of Neva and the tempest's sound
Rang in his ears. Silent, obsessed
With dreadful thoughts, he roamed around.
Some dream tormented his mind's eye.
Although a week, a month went by
They never saw him homeward-bound.
His empty, cosy room was hired,
The day the landlord's time expired,
To some poor poet. His things neglected   360
Yevgeny never came to claim.
A stranger, by the world rejected,
All day he wandered without aim,
Sleeping on quays; for food he found
Odd morsels on some window-sill.
He wore the same poor clothing still,
All torn and rotting. At his back
Stone-throwing hooligans would play.
The coachman's whip would often crack
And lash him as he made his way,   370
A figure on the highroad, blind,
Oblivious to all around,
It seemed, and deafened by the sound
Of terrors ringing in his mind,
Thus dragging out his sorry span,
Akin to neither beast nor man,
Not anything, not earthly stuff,
Not lifeless spirit . . .
                            Once he slept
Down by the Neva dockside. Rough
Breathed out the wind, as summer crept   380
To autumn. Sombre billows leapt

And foamed and moaned upon the docks
On velvet steps, like one who knocks
At judges' doors to press his case,
Ignored by them in every place.
He woke, poor creature, to the dark
And drizzle; a sad wind howled, and hark!
The watchman's cry out yonder might
Be an echo called across the night . . .
Yevgeny gave a start; appalled   390
By horrors vividly recalled,
He leapt up, set off roaming, then
Quite suddenly he stopped again
And slowly looked around and cowered,
His face distorted wild with fear.
A mansion house above him towered,
A great big house with columns. Here,
Raising a paw, above the entry,
Lifelike, the lions stood on sentry,
And in the darkness, high indeed   400
Above the rock and railing, why!
One arm outflung across the sky,
The Idol straddled his bronze steed.

Yevgeny shuddered. Horribly clear
His thoughts had grown. For now he knew
This place the floods had sported through,
Where grasping waves had crowded near,
All round, rebellious and grim,
Those lions, and the square, and Him,
Towering high, unmoving. He,   410
Whose bronze head crowned the darkness still,
Had founded by his fateful will
This city by the very sea . . .
Fearsome in all the darkness now!
What contemplation in that brow!
What strength and sinew in him hidden!
And in that horse what fiery speed!

Where do you gallop, haughty steed?
Where will those falling hooves be ridden?

O mighty overlord of Fate!   420
With iron curb, on high, like this,
Did you not raise on the abyss
Our Russia to her rampant state?

This poor, demented creature here
Went walking round the Idol's base;
His wild eyes sought and found the face
Of him who ruled a hemisphere.
He felt a tightness in his breast,
Against the chilly railing pressed
His brow. His misted eyes were staring;   430
He felt a boiling in his blood,
A blazing in his heart. He stood
Before the proud colossus, glaring,
With gritted teeth and fingers crushed,
Like one with evil powers filled;
'You, and the miracles you build!'
He hissed, and shook, angrily flushed,
'I'll have you . . .' Then away he rushed
Headlong, all of a sudden discerning
The dreaded Tsar, – or so he thought –   440
In a flash of mounting fury caught,
And softly, slowly, his face was turning . . .
    And out across the empty square
He runs; behind him, he would swear,
A crashing roll of thunder moves,
Of ringing and resounding hooves
Upon the quaking thoroughfare.
And, splendid in the pale moonlight,
One arm flung out on high, full speed,
Comes the Bronze Horseman in his flight,   450
Upon his crashing, clanging steed.
The poor mad creature! All that night,
No matter where his footsteps led,
Still the Bronze Horseman in his flight
Leapt on behind with heavy tread.

From that time on, when chance directed
That he should walk the square again,

Uneasiness would be reflected
Upon his face. Hurriedly, then,
A hand upon his heart he pressed   460
To still the torture in his breast;
His tattered, shabby cap was doffed;
Eyes worried, never raised aloft,
He edged along.
              An islet stands
Close by the shore. Late at his trade,
Sometimes a fisherman, delayed,
Comes with his fishing-net and lands
To cook his frugal supper. Or
Some office-worker comes ashore
Upon the island-waste, out rowing   470
On Sunday. Not a single blade
Of grass has grown there. Freely flowing,
The floods washed up here, as they played,
A mean old shack. There it survived,
A black bush darkening the deep.
One day last spring a barge arrived
And took it off, a ruined heap,
Deserted. Near the door they found
My madman. As the Lord ordains,
They gathered up his cold remains   480
And there they laid them in the ground.

                       (1833)

Acknowledgements

The editor and publishers wish to thank the following for
permission to use copyright material:

Faber and Faber Ltd for Alexander Pushkin 'The Caucasus', from *Poems
from the Russian*, trans. Frances Cornfield and Esther Polianowsky, 1943;

Macmillan Publishers for poems by Alexander Pushkin translated by
C. M. Bowra included in *A Second Book of Russian Verse*, ed. C. M. Bowra,
Macmillan & Co. Ltd, 1948.

Every effort has been made to trace the copyright holders but if any have
been inadvertently overlooked the publishers will be pleased to make the
necessary arrangement at the first opportunity.

Everyman's Poetry

Titles available in this series